POACHERS AND POACHING

"Knowledge never learned in schools."

POACHERS AND POACHING

BY

JOHN WATSON, F.L.S.

AUTHOR OF
"NATURE AND WOODCRAFT," "SYLVAN FOLK," "BRITISH SPORTING FISHES,"
EDITOR OF "THE CONFESSIONS OF A POACHER."

With a Frontispiece

LONDON: CHAPMAN AND HALL
LIMITED
1891

[*All Rights reserved*]

WESTMINSTER:
PRINTED BY NICHOLS AND SONS,
25, PARLIAMENT STREET.

NOTE.

These chapters originally appeared as articles in *Macmillan's Magazine,* the *Cornhill Magazine,* the *National Review,* the *Gentleman's Magazine,* the *St. James's Gazette* and the *Pall Mall Gazette;* and I have to thank the Editors and Proprietors of these periodicals for permission to reprint them. The chapter entitled "Water Poachers" is reprinted by permission from the *Nineteenth Century.*

As to the facts in the volume, they are mainly taken at first hand from nature.

J. W.

CONTENTS.

CHAPTER I.
POACHERS AND POACHING.—I. 1

CHAPTER II.
POACHERS AND POACHING.—II. 17

CHAPTER III.
BADGERS AND OTTERS 33

CHAPTER IV.
COURIERS OF THE AIR 44

CHAPTER V.
THE SNOW-WALKERS 86

CHAPTER VI.
WHEN DARKNESS HAS FALLEN 94

Contents.

PAGE

CHAPTER VII.
BRITISH BIRDS, THEIR NESTS AND EGGS . . 118

CHAPTER VIII.
MINOR BRITISH GAME BIRDS 143

CHAPTER IX.
WATER POACHERS 162

CHAPTER X.
WILD DUCKS AND DUCK DECOYING . . . 195

CHAPTER XI.
FIELD AND COVERT POACHERS 223

CHAPTER XII.
HOMELY TRAGEDY 245

CHAPTER XIII.
WORKERS IN WOODCRAFT 266

CHAPTER XIV.
SKETCHES FROM NATURE 287

POACHERS AND POACHING.

CHAPTER I.

POACHERS AND POACHING.—I.

THE poacher is a product of sleepy village life, and usually "mouches" on the outskirts of country towns. His cottage is roughly adorned in fur and feather, and abuts on the fields. There is a fitness in this, and an appropriateness in the two gaunt lurchers stretched before the door. These turn day into night on the sunny roadside in summer, and before the cottage fire in winter. Like the poacher, they are active and silent when the village community is asleep.

Our Bohemian has poached time out of mind. His family have been poachers for generations. The county justices, the magistrates' clerk, the county constable, and the gaol books all testify to the same fact.

The poacher's lads have grown up under their father's tuition, and follow in his footsteps. Even now they are inveterate poachers, and have a special instinct for capturing field-mice and squirrels. They take moles in their runs, and preserve their skins. When a number of these are collected they are sold to the labourers' wives, who make them into vests. In wheat-time the farmers employ the lads to keep down sparrows and finches. Numbers of larks are taken in nooses, and in spring lapwings' eggs yield quite a rich harvest from the uplands and ploughed fields. A shilling so earned is to the young poacher riches indeed ; money so acquired is looked upon differently from that earned by steady-going labour on the field or farm. In their season he gathers cresses and blackberries, the embrowned nuts constituting an autumn in themselves. Snipe and woodcock, which come to the marshy meadows in severe weather, are taken in "gins" and "springes." Traps are laid for wild ducks in the runners when the still mountain tarns are frozen over. When our poacher's lads attain to sixteen they become in turn the owner of an old flintlock, an heirloom, which has been in the family for generations. Then larger game can be got at. Wood-pigeons are waited for in the larches, and shot as they come to roost. Large numbers of plover are bagged from time to time, both green and grey. These feed in the water meadows through autumn and winter, and are always plentiful. In spring the rare dotterels were sometimes shot as they stayed on their way to the hills; or a gaunt heron was brought down as it flew heavily from a ditch. To the now disused mill-dam ducks came on wintry evening—teal, mallard, and pochards. The lad lay coiled up behind a willow root, and waited during the night. Soon the whistling of wings was heard, and dark forms appeared against the skyline. The old duck-gun was out, a sharp report tore the darkness, and a brace of teal floated down stream and washed on to the mill island. In this way half-a-dozen ducks would be bagged, and dead or dying were left where they fell, and retrieved next morning. Sometimes big game was obtained in the shape of a brace of wild geese, the least wary of a flock; but these only came in the severest weather.

At night the poacher's dogs embody all his senses. An old black bitch is his favourite; for years she has served him faithfully—in the whole of that time never having once given mouth. Like all good lurchers, she is bred between the greyhound and sheepdog. The produce of this cross have the speed of the one, and the "nose" and intelligence of the other.

Such dogs never bark, and, being rough coated, are able to stand the exposure of cold nights. They take long to train, but when perfected are invaluable to the poacher. Upon them almost wholly depends success.

Poaching is one of the fine arts, and the most successful poacher is always a specialist. He selects one kind of game, and his whole knowledge of woodcraft is directed against it. In autumn and winter the "Otter" knows the whereabouts of every hare in the parish; not only the field in which it is but the very clump of rushes in which is its "form." As puss goes away from the prickly gorse bush, or flies down the turnip "rigg," he notes her every twist and double, and takes in the minutest details. He is also careful to examine the "smoots" and gates through which she passes, and these spots he always approaches laterally. He leaves no scent of hand nor print of foot, and does not disturb rough herbage. Late afternoon brings him home, and upon the clean sanded floor his wires and nets are spread. There is a peg to sharpen and a broken mesh to mend. Every now and then he looks out upon the darkening night, always directing his glance upward. His dogs whine impatiently to be gone. In an hour, with bulky pockets, he starts, striking across the land and away from the highroad. The dogs prick out their ears upon the track, but stick doggedly to his heels. After a while the darkness blots out even the forms of surrounding objects, and the poacher moves more cautiously. A couple of snares are set in holes in an old thorn fence not more than a yard apart. These are delicately manipulated, and from previous knowledge the poacher knows that the hare will take one of them. The black dog is sent over, the younger fawn bitch staying with her master. The former slinks slowly down the field, sticking closely to the cover of a fence running at right angles to the one in which the wires are set. The poacher has arranged that the wind shall blow from the dog and across the hare's seat when the former shall come opposite. The ruse acts, and puss is alarmed but not terrified; she gets up and goes quietly away for the hedge. The dog is crouched and anxiously watching her; she is making right for the snare, though something must be added to her speed to make the wire effective. As the dog closes in, the poacher, bowed, and with hands on knees, waits, still as death, for her coming. He hears the trip, trip, trip, as the herbage is brushed; there is a rustle among the leaves, a momentary squeal—and the wire has tightened round her throat.

Again the three trudge silently along the lane. Suddenly the trio stop and listen; then they disperse, but seem to have dissolved. The dry ditch is capacious, and its dead herbage tall and tangled. A heavy foot, with regular beat, approaches along the road, and dies slowly away in the distance.

Hares love green corn stalks, and a field of young wheat is at hand. A net, twelve feet by six, is spread at the gate, and at a given sign the dogs depart different ways. Their paths would seem soon to have converged, for the night is torn by a piteous cry, the road is enveloped in dust, and in the midst of the confusion the dogs dash over the fence. They must have found their game near the middle of the field, and driven the hares—for there are two—so hard that they carried the net right before them. Every struggle wraps another mesh about them, and soon their screams are quieted. By a quick movement the poacher wraps the long net about his arm, and, taking the noiseless sward, gets hastily away from the spot. These are the common methods of hare-poaching.

In March, when they are pairing, four or five may often be found together in one field. Although wild, they seem to lose much of their natural timidity, and now the poacher reaps a rich harvest. He is careful to set his nets and snares on the side *opposite* to that from which the game will come, for this reason: That hares approach any place through which they are about to pass in a zig-zag manner. They come on, playing and frisking, stopping now and then to nibble the sweet herbage. They run, making wide leaps at right angles to their path, and sit listening upon their haunches. A freshly-impressed foot-mark, the scent of dog or man at the gate, almost invariably turns them back. Of course these traces are necessarily left if the snare be set on the *near* side of the gate or fence, and then they refuse to take it even when hard pressed. Where poaching is prevalent and hares abundant, the keepers net every one on the estate, for it is well known to those versed in woodcraft that an escaped hare once netted can never be taken a second time in the same manner. The human scent left at gaps and gateways by ploughmen and shepherds the wary poacher will obliterate by driving sheep over the spot before he begins operations. On the sides of the fells and uplands hares are difficult to kill. This can only be accomplished by swift dogs, which are taken *above* the game; puss is made to run down hill, when, from her peculiar formation, she goes at a disadvantage.

Our poacher is cooly audacious. Here is an actual incident. There was a certain field of young wheat in which were some hares. The knowledge of these came by observation during the day. The field was hard by the Keeper's cottage, and surrounded by a high fence of loose stones. The situation was therefore critical, but that night nets were set at the gates through which the hares always made. To drive them the dog was to range the field, entering it at a point furthest away from the gate. Silence was essential to success. To aid the dog, the poacher bent his back in the road at a yard from the wall. The dog retired, took a mighty spring, and, barely touching his master's shoulders, bounded over the fence without touching. From that field five hares were killed.

It need hardly be remarked that the intelligent poacher is always a naturalist. The signs of wind and weather he knows as it were by heart, and this is essential to his silent trade. The rise and wane of the moon, the rain-bringing tides, the local migration of birds—these and a hundred other things are marked in his unwritten calendar. His out-door life has made him quick and taught him of much ready animal ingenuity. He has imbibed an immense amount of knowledge of the life of the woods and fields, and he is that one man in a thousand who has accuracy of eye and judgment sufficient to interpret nature aright.

It has been already remarked that the poacher is nothing if not a specialist. As yet we have spoken only of the "moucher" who directs his attention to fur. But if there is less scope for field ingenuity in the taking of some of our game birds, there is always the possibility of more wholesale destruction. This arises from the fact of the birds being gregarious. Partridges roost close to the ground, and sleep with their heads tucked together. A covey in this position represents little more than a mass of feathers. They always spend their nights in the open, for protective reasons. Birds which do not perch would soon be extinct as a species were they to seek the protection of woods and hedge-bottoms by night. Such ground generally affords cover to vermin—weasels, polecats, and stoats. Although partridges roam far by day, they always come together at night, being partial to the same fields and fallows. They run much, and rarely fly except when passing from one feeding ground to another. In coming together in the evening their calls may be heard at some distance. These sounds the poacher listens for and marks. He remembers the nest under the gorse bush, and knows that the covey will not be far distant.

Partridges the poacher considers good game. He may watch half-a-dozen coveys at once. Each evening at sun-down he goes his rounds and makes mental notes. Three coveys are marked for a night's work—one in turnips, another among stubble, and a third on grass. At dark he comes and now requires an assistant. The net is dragged along the ground, and as the birds get up it is simply dropped over them, when usually the whole covey is taken. In view of this method of poaching and on land where many partridges roost, low scrubby thorns are planted at regular intervals. These so far interfere with the working of the net as to allow the birds time to escape. If the poacher has not accurately marked down his game beforehand, a much wider net is needed. Among turnips, and where large numbers of birds are supposed to lie, several rows or "riggs" are taken at a time, until the whole of the ground has been traversed. This last method requires time and a knowledge of the keeper's beat. On rough ground the catching of the net may be obviated by having about eighteen inches of smooth glazed material bordering the lower and trailing part of the net. Partridges are occasionally taken by farmers in the following unorthodox fashion. A train of grain is scattered from ground where game is known to lie. The birds follow this, and each morning find it more nearly approach to the stackyards. When the birds have become accustomed to this mode of feeding, the grain train is continued inside the barn. The birds follow, and the doors are closed upon them. A bright light is brought, and the game is knocked down with sticks.

Partridges feed in the early morning—as soon as daybreak. They resort to one spot, and are constant in their coming if encouraged. This the poacher knows, and adapts himself accordingly. By the aid of a clear moon he lays a train of grain straight as a hazel stick. He has brought in a bag an old duck-gun, the barrels of which are short, having been filed down. This short weapon can easily be carried in his capacious pocket, and is only needed to fire at short distances. Into this he crams a heavy charge of powder and waits for the dawn. The covey comes with a loud whirring of wings, and the birds settle to feed immediately. Firing along the line, a single shot strews the ground with dead and dying. In ten minutes he is a mile from the spot, always keeping clear of the roads. The poacher has yet another method. Grain is soaked until it becomes swollen and is then steeped in the strongest spirit. This, as before, is strewn in the morning paths of the partridge, and, soon taking effect, the naturally pugnacious birds are presently staggering and fighting desperately. The poacher bides his time, and, as opportunity offers, knocks the incapacitated birds on the head.

The wilder grouse poaching of the moorlands is now rarely followed. The birds are taken in nets similar to those used for partridges. By imitating the peculiar gurgling call-notes of the grouse, old poachers can bring up all birds within hearing distance. As they fly over the knolls and braes they are shot. Many of the birds sold in London on the morning of the "Twelfth" are taken in this way. In the north, since the inclosure of the Commons, numbers of grouse are killed by flying against the wire fences. When the mists cling to the hills for days, or when the weather is "thick," these casualties occur. At such times the birds fly low, and strike before seeing the obstacle. The poacher notes these mist caps hanging to the hill tops, and then, bag in hand, walks parallel to miles and miles of fence. Sometimes a dozen brace of birds are picked up in a morning. Not only grouse, but on the lowlands pheasants and partridges are killed in this way, as are also snipe and woodcock.

In summer, poachers make and repair their nets for winter use. Large hare nets are made for gates, and smaller ones for rabbit burrows and "smoots." Partridge nets are also necessarily large, having sometimes to cover half a field. Although most of the summer the poacher is practically idle, it is at this time that he closely studies the life of the fields, and makes his observations for winter. He gets occasional employment at hay or harvest, and for his darker profession treasures up what he sees. He is not often introduced to the heart of the land, and misses nothing of the opportunity. On in autumn, he is engaged to cut down ash poles or fell young woods, and this brings him to the covert. Nothing escapes his notice, and in the end his employers have to pay dearly for his labour. At this time the game birds—pheasants, partridge, and grouse—are breeding, and are therefore worthless; so with rabbits and hares. But when game is "out," fish are "in." Fish poaching has decreased of late years, owing to stricter watching and greater preservation generally. In summer, when the waters are low, fish resort to the deep dubs. In such spots comes abundance of food, and the fish are safe, be the drought never so long. The pools of the Fell becks abound at such times with speckled brown trout, and are visited by another poacher—the otter. When the short summer night is darkest, the man poacher wades through the meadows by the river. He knows the deeps where the fish most congregate, and there throws in chloride of lime. Soon the trout of the pool float belly uppermost, and are lifted out, dazed, in a landing net. In this way hundreds of fish are taken, and find a ready sale. The lime in no wise poisons the edible parts; it simply affects the eyes and gills, covering them with a fine white film. Fish so taken, however, lose all their pinky freshness. The most cowardly part of this not uncommon proceeding is that the lime is sometimes put into the river immediately below a mill. This, of course, is intended to mislead watchers and keepers, and to throw the blame upon the non-guilty millowner. And, seeing that chloride of lime is used in various manufactures, the ruse sometimes succeeds. Many of the older poachers, however, discountenance this cowardly method, for by it the destruction of fish is wholesale, irrespective of size. The old hands use an old-fashioned net, to work which requires at least two men. The net is dragged along the quiet river reaches, a rope being attached to each end. The trout fly before it, and are drawn out upon the first bed of pebbles. In this way great hauls are often made. To prevent this species of poaching, stakes are driven into trout stream beds; but they are not of much avail. When it is known that a "reach" is staked, a third man wades behind the net and lifts it over. A better method to prevent river poaching is to throw loose thorn bushes into the bed of the stream. In trailing along the bottom the net becomes entangled, and long before it can be unloosed the fish have escaped. This wholesale instrument of fish poaching is now rarely used. The net is necessarily large and cumbersome. Wet, it is as much as two men can carry, and when caught in the act, there is nothing for it but to abandon the net and run. This is an effectual check for a time, as a new net takes long to knit and is expensive, at least to the poacher. When salmon and trout are spawning their senses seem somewhat dulled, and they are taken out of the water at night by click-hooks. In this kind of river poaching a lighted tar brand is used to show the whereabouts of the fish. A light, too, attracts salmon. Of course, this can only be attempted when the beats of the watchers and keepers are known. The older generation of poachers, who have died or are fast dying out, seem to have taken the receipt for preparing salmon roe with them. For this once deadly bait is now rarely used. Here is a field incident.

A silent river reach shaded by trees. It is the end of a short summer night. We know that the poachers have lately been busy knitting their nets, and have come to intercept them. The "Alder Dub" may be easily netted, and contains a score nice trout. Poachers carefully study the habits of fish as well as those of game, both winged and furred. To the alder dub they know the trout make when the river is low. The poachers have not noted signs of wind and weather and of local migrations for twenty years past to be ignorant of this. And so here, in the dew-beaded grass, we lie in wait. It is two o'clock and a critical time. A strange breaking is in the east: grey—half-light, half-mist. If they come they will come now. In an hour the darkness will not hide them. We lie close to the bank thickly covered with bush and scrub. Two sounds are and have been heard all night—the ceaseless call of the crake and the not less ceaseless song of the sedge-bird.

A lapwing gets up in the darkness and screams —an ominous sound, and we are all ear. Three forms descend the opposite bank, and on to the gravel bed. They empty the contents of a bag and begin to unroll its slow length. The breaking of a rotten twig in a preparatory movement for the rush sufficiently alarms them, and they dash into the wood as we into the water— content now to secure their cumbersome illegal net, and thus effectually stop their operations for three weeks at least. The grey becomes dawn and the dawn light as we wade wearily home through the long wet grass. And still the sedge warbler sings.

CHAPTER II.

POACHERS AND POACHING.—II.

THE confines of a large estate constitute a poacher's paradise; for although partridge and grouse require land suited to their taste, rabbits and pheasants are common to all preserved ground. Since the reclamation of much wild land these latter afford his chief spoil. And then rabbits may be taken at any time of the year and in so many different ways. They are abundant, too, and always find a ready market. The penalties attached to rabbit poaching are less than those of game, and the vermin need not be followed into closely preserved coverts. The extermination of the rabbit will be contemporaneous with that of the lurcher and poacher—two institutions of English village life which date back to the planting the New Forest. Of the many modes of taking the "coney," ferreting and field-netting are the most common. Traps with steel jaws are sometimes set in their runs, and are inserted in the turf so as to bring them level with the sward. But destruction by this method is not sufficiently wholesale, and the upturned white under parts show too plainly against the green. The poacher's methods must be quick, and he cannot afford to visit by day traps set in the dark. When the unscrupulous keeper finds a snare he sometimes puts a leveret into it, and secretes himself. He then waits, and captures the poacher "in the act." As with some other methods already mentioned, the trap poacher is only a casual. Ferreting is silent and usually successful. In warrens, both inequalities of the ground and mounds and ditches afford cover for the poacher. A tangled hedge bank with tunnellings and coarse herbage is always a favourite spot. There are generally two and often half-a-dozen holes in the same burrow. Small purse nets are spread over these, and the poacher prefers them loose to being pegged or fixed in any way. When the nets are set the ferrets are taken from the moucher's capacious pockets and turned in. They do not proceed immediately, but sniff the mouth of the hole; their decision is only momentary for soon the tips of their tails disappear in the darkness. Now, above all times, silence is essential. Rabbits refuse to bolt if there is noise outside. A dull thud, a rush, and a rabbit goes rolling over and over entangled in the net; one close after it gets clear away. Reserve nets are quickly clapped to the holes as the rabbits bolt, these invariably being taken, except where a couple come together. Standing on the mound a shot would stop these as they go bounding through the dead leaves; but this would bring up the keeper, and so the poacher practices self-denial. Unlike hares, rabbits rarely squeal when they become entangled; and this allows the poacher to ferret long and silently. Rabbits that refuse to take the net are sometimes eaten into by the ferret, but still refuse to bolt. If a rabbit makes along a blind burrow followed by a ferret, the former is killed, and the latter gluts itself upon the body. When this occurs it is awkward for the poacher; the ferret in such case usually curls itself up and goes to sleep; left to itself it might stay in the hole for days; and so it has either to be dug or starved out. Both processes are long, the burrows ramify far into the bank, and it is not certainly known in which the ferret remains.

The poacher's wholesale method of night poaching for rabbits is by means of two long nets. These are set parallel to each other along the edge of a wood, and about thirty yards out into the field or pasture. Only about four inches divides the nets. A clear star-lit night is best for the work, and at the time the nets are set the ground game is far out feeding. The nets are long—the first small in mesh, that immediately behind it large. When a hare or rabbit strikes, the impetus takes a part of the first net and its contents through the larger mesh of the second, and there hanging, the creature struggles until it is knocked on the head with a stick. Immediately the nets are set two men and a couple of lurchers begin to range the ground in front— slowly and patiently, gradually driving every feeding thing woodwards. A third man quietly paces the sward behind the nets, killing whatever game strikes them. And in this way hundreds of rabbits may be, and are, taken in a single night. Some years ago half-a-dozen young rabbits appeared in our meadow-lot which were of the ordinary grey with large white patches. Whilst feeding these stood out conspicuously from the rest; they were religiously preserved. Of these parti-coloured ones a normal number is now kept up, and as poachers rarely discriminate, whenever they disappear, it is *primâ facie* evidence that night work is going on.

Of all poaching that of pheasants is the most beset with difficulty ; and the pheasant poacher is usually a desperate character. Many methods can be successfully employed, and the pheasant is rather a stupid bird. Its one great characteristic is that of wandering, and this cannot be prevented. Although fed daily, and with the daintiest food, the birds, singly or in pairs, may frequently be seen far from the home covers.

Of course the poacher knows this, and is quick to use his knowledge. It by no means follows that the man who rears the pheasants will have the privilege of shooting them. In autumn, when beechmast and acorns begin to fall, the pheasants make daily journeys in search of them; and of these they consume great quantities. They feed principally in the morning, dust themselves in the turnip-fields at noon, and ramble through the woods in the afternoon; and when wandered birds find themselves in outlying copses in the evening they are apt to roost there.

It need hardly be said that pheasants are generally reared close to the keeper's cottage; that their coverts immediately surround it. Most commonly it is a gang of armed ruffians that enter these, and not the country poacher. Then there are reasons for this. Opposition must always be anticipated, for the covert should never be, and rarely is, unwatched. And then there are the results of capture to be taken into account. This effected, and with birds in his possession, the poacher is liable to be indicted upon so many charges, each and all having heavy penalties.

When wholesale pheasant poaching is prosecuted by gangs, it is in winter, when the trees are bare. Guns, the barrels of which are filed down so as to shorten them, are taken in sacks, and the birds are shot where they roost. Their bulky forms stand sharply outlined against the sky, and they are often on the lower branches. If the firing does not immediately bring up the keepers, the game is quickly deposited in bags and the gang makes off. It not unfrequently happens that a light cart is waiting to receive the men at some grassy lane end. But the moucher obtains his game in a quieter way. He eschews the preserves, and looks up outlying birds. He always carries a pocketful of corn, and day by day entices the birds further and further away. This accomplished he may snare them : and take them in iron traps. He sometimes uses a gun, but only when other methods have failed. A common and successful way he has is to light brimstone beneath the trees in which the pheasants roost. The powerful fumes soon overpower the birds, and they come flapping down the trees one by one. This method has the advantage of silence, and if the night is still need not be detected. Away from the preserves time is no object, and so the moucher who works systematically, and is content with a brace of birds at a time, usually gets the most in the end, with least chance of capture. The pugnacity of the pheasant is well known to him, and out of this trait he makes capital. When the whereabouts of the keeper is known, he takes under his arm a game cock fitted with artificial spurs. These are attached to the natural ones, are sharp as needles, and the bird is trained how to use them. Upon the latter's crowing one or more cock pheasants immediately respond and advance to meet the adversary. A single blow usually suffices to lay low the pride of the pheasant, and in this way half a-dozen birds may often be taken whilst the poacher's representative remains unhurt.

The most cruelly ingenious plan adopted by poachers, however, is also one of the most successful. If time and opportunity offer, there is scarcely any limit to the depredations which it allows. A number of dried peas are taken and steeped in boiling water; a hole is then made through the centre with a needle or some sharp instrument, and through this a stiff bristle is threaded. The ends are cut off short, leaving only about a quarter of an inch of bristle projecting at each end. With these the birds are fed, and are greedily eaten. In passing down the gullet, however, a violent irritation is set up, and the pheasant is finally choked.

The birds are picked up in a dying condition from beneath the hedges, to which shelter they almost always run. The plan is a quiet one; may be adopted in roads and lanes where the birds dust themselves, and does not require trespass.

The methods here set forth both with regard to pheasants and rabbits are those ordinarily in use. In connection with the former it might have been remarked that the gamekeeper sometimes outwits the poacher by a device which is now of old standing. Knowing well from what quarter the depredators will enter the woods, wooden blocks representing roosting birds are nailed to the branches of the open beeches. The poacher rarely fires at these "dummies," and it is only with the casual that the ruse works. He fires, brings the keepers out of their hiding places and so is entrapped.

It need hardly be said that our poacher is a compound of many individuals—the type of a numerous class. The tinge of rustic romance to which we have already referred as exhibited in his character may have been detected in his goings. And we may at once say that he in nowise resembles the armed ruffian who, masked and with murderous intent, enters the covert at night. Although his life is one long protest against the game laws, he is not without a rude code of morality. He complains bitterly of the decrease of game, and that the profession is hardly now worth following. Endowed with marked intelligence, it has never been directed aright. His knowledge of woodcraft is superior to that of the gamekeeper, which personage he holds in contempt. He quietly boasts of having outwitted the keepers a hundred times. The "Otter" is chary as to those he takes into confidence, and knows that silence is essential to success. He points to the "Mole,"—the mouldy *sobriquet* of a compatriot—as an instance of one who tells poaching secrets to village gossips. The "Mole" spends most of his time in the county gaol, and is now undergoing incarceration for the fifty-seventh time. Our "Otter" has certainly been caught, but the occasions of his capture form but a small percentage of the times he has been "out." He is a healthy example of pure animalism, and his rugged nature has much in common with the animals and birds. As an accurately detailed reflection of nature, his monograph of any one of our British game-birds would excel even those of Mr. Jefferies himself; yet of culture he hasn't an idea. He admires the pencilled plumage of a dead woodcock, and notes how marvellously it conforms to the grey-brown herbage among which it lies. So, too, with the eggs of birds. He remarks on the conformation to environment — of partridge and pheasant, the olive colour to the dead oak leaves; of snipe and plover to the mottled marsh; of duck and water fowl to the pale green reeds.

As to his morality with regard to the game laws, it would be difficult to detect exactly where he draws the line. He lives for these to be repealed, but his native philosophy tells him that when this time comes game will have become well nigh extinct. Upon the Ground Game Act he looks with mingled feelings, for, after all, are not rabbits and hares the chief product of his nights? The farmers now get these, and the poacher's field is limited. They engage him, maybe, to stay the ravages upon clover and young wheat, or to thin the rabbits from out the pastures. He propitiates the farmer in many ways. Occasionally in the morning the farm lad finds half-a-dozen rabbits or a hare dropped behind the barn door. How these came there no one knows—nor asks. The country attorney is sometimes submitted to a like indignity. In crossing land the poacher is careful to close gates after him, and he never breaks down fences. He assists cattle and sheep which he finds in extremity, and leaves word of the mishap at the farm. Is it likely that the farmer will dog the steps of the man who protects his property, and pays tolls for doing it?

And it frequently happens that the poacher is not less popular with the village community at large than with those whose interests he serves. It is even asserted that more than one of the county Justices have, in some sort, a sneaking affection for him. The same wild spirit and love of sport take him to the fields and woods as his more fortunate brethren to the moor and covert. It is untrue, as has been said, that the poacher is always a mercenary wretch who invariably sells his game; he as frequently sends in a brace of birds or a hare to a poor or sick neighbour. He comes in contact with the law just sufficient to make him know something of its bearings. When charged with being in possession of "game," he reiterates the old argument that rabbits are vermin. Being committed for four months "for night poaching," he respectfully informs the presiding Justice that at the time of his capture the sun had risen two hours, and that the law does not allow more than half the sentence just passed upon him. The old clerk fumbles for his horn spectacles, and, after turning over *Stone's Justices' Manual* solemnly informs the Bench that defendant in his interpretation is right. He remembers this little episode and chuckles over it. There is another which is equally marked in his memory. The "Otter" poached long and successfully ere he was caught, and then was driven into an ambuscade by a combination of keepers. Exultant at his downfall, the men of gaiters flocked from every estate in the country-side to witness his conviction. Some, who had only seen a vanishing form in the darkness, attended to see the man. This wild spirit of the night was always followed by an old black bitch. She, too, was produced in court, and was an object of much curiosity. The "Otter" had been taken in the act, he told the Bench. "He deserved no quarter and asked none. Poaching was right by the Bible, but wrong by the Law." One of the Justices deigned to remark it was a question of "property," not morality. "Oh!" rejoined the "Otter," "because blue blood doesn't run in my veins, that's no reason why I shouldn't have my share." And after a moment's pause : " But its a queer kind o' property that's yours in that field, mine in the turnpike, and a third man's over the next fence."

The end of it was, however, a fine of £5, with an alternative. And so the case ended. But that day the keepers and their assistants had forgotten the first principles of watching. The best keeper is the one that is least seen. Only let the poacher know his whereabouts, and the latter's work is easy. It was afterwards remarked that during the trial of the "Otter" not a poacher was in court. This fact in itself was unusual—and significant. It became more so when he was released by reason of his heavy fine being paid the same evening. More than one woman had been seen labouring under loaded baskets near the local game dealer's, and these were innocently covered with mantling cresses, and so at the time escaped suspicion. Upon this memorable day the pheasants had been fed by unseen hands and had vanished. The only traces left by the covert side were fluffy feathers everywhere.

Few hares remained on the land; these had either been snared or netted at the gates. The rabbits' burrows had been ferreted, an outhouse near the keeper's cottage being entered to obtain possession of the ferrets. It need hardly be said that had the "Otter" been aware he would not have countenanced these lawless doings of his *confrères*. He claimed to "poach square," and drew the line at home-reared pheasants, allowing them "property." Those he found wild in the woods, however, were *feræ naturæ*, and he directed his engines accordingly.

Every poacher knows that the difficulty lies not so much in obtaining the game as in transporting it safely home. Their dogs are always trained to run on a couple of hundred yards in advance, so as to give warning of anyone's approach. If a police constable or keeper is met on the highway the dog immediately leaps the fence, and, under its cover, runs back to its master. Seeing this the game-bag is dropped into a dry ditch, and dog and man make off in different directions. County constables loiter about unfrequented lanes and by-paths at daybreak. The poachers know this and are rarely met with game upon them. Ditches, stacks, and ricks afford good hiding places until women can be sent to fetch the spoil. These failing, country carriers and morning milk carts are useful to the poacher.

In one sleepy village known to us both the rural postman and the parish clerk were poachers. The latter carried his game in the black bag which usually held the funeral pall. The smith at the shoeing forge was a regular receiver, and there were few in the village who had not poached at some time or other. The cottage women netted fish, and shut the garden gates on hares and rabbits when they came down to feed in winter. Upon one occasion a poacher, taking advantage of a country funeral, had himself and a large haul taken to the nearest market town, the hearse disgorging its questionable corpse behind the nearest game shop. Another of the poachers, nicknamed the " gentleman," was wont to attire himself in broad-brimmed hat and frock coat similar to those worn a century ago by the people called Quakers. In the former he carried his nets, and in the capacious pockets of the latter the game he took. These outward guarantees of good faith away from his own parish precluded him from ever once being searched.

Of late years egg poaching has been reduced to a science; and this is one of the worst phases of the whole subject. In certain districts it is carried on to a large extent, and comes of artificial rearing. The squire's keeper will give six pence each for pheasants' eggs and four pence for those of partridges. He often buys eggs (unknowingly, of course) from his own preserves, as well as from those of his neighbours. In the hedge bottom, along the covert side, or among gorse and broom, the poacher notices a pair of partridges roaming morning after morning. Soon he finds their oak-leaf nest and olive eggs. These the keeper readily buys; winking at what he knows to be dishonest. Plough-boys and farm-labourers have peculiar opportunities for egg-poaching. As to pheasants' eggs, if the keeper is an honest man and refuses to buy, there are always London dealers who will. Once in the covert, pheasants' eggs are easily found. The birds get up heavily from their nests, and go away with a loud whirring of wings. In this species of poaching women and children are largely employed. At the time the former are ostensibly gathering sticks, the latter wild flowers. A receiver has been known to send to London in the course of a week a thousand eggs—probably every one of them stolen.

When depredations are carried on nightly, or game disappears in large quantities, warrants are obtained, and search made for nets. Except for immediate use the poachers seldom keep their nets at home. They are stowed away in church tower, barn, rick, or out-house. Upon one occasion it got abroad that the constables would make a raid upon a certain cottage where a large net was known to be. The dwelling was a disused toll bar on the turnpike, and commanded a long stretch of road. The good woman of the house saw the constables approaching, and made the most of her time. Taking off her gown, she fastened one end of the net, which was long and narrow, to a projecting crook in the wall; then retiring to the further side of the kitchen, she attached the other end of it to the whalebone of her stays, and by turning round and round, wound the net about her capacious person. When the constables arrived she accompanied them into every corner of the cottage, but no net could be found.

CHAPTER III.

BADGERS AND OTTERS.

HAZELHURST was a long line of woodland, on one side skirted by the sea and on the other by a crumbling limestone escarpment. It was woodland, too, with the deep impress of time upon it—a forest primeval. The branches and boles of the oaks were tortured out of all original conception. Save for colour they might have been congealed water or duramen muscles. Down in the hollows there was deep moss, elastic and silent, over all. For centuries the pines had shed their needles undisturbed. These and the pine trunks sent up a sweet savour from the earth—an odour that acted as a tonic to the whole being. There were sun-flashes in the glades, where the jays chattered and the cushats cooed, and where ever and anon a rabbit rustled through. Often over these the kestrel hung and vibrated its shadow on the spot beneath; or the sparrow-hawk with its clean-cut figure stared with the down on his beak on a dead pine bough. In the summer red creatures that were bits of light gracefully glided among green tassels, and the chatter of squirrels was heard. The older trees attracted woodpeckers, and the nuthatch threw out fine fibres of rotten wood. Sometimes a pheasant or a partridge would startle, getting up from its olive eggs by a log left by the charcoal-burners. Thus rudely disturbed, it had no time to scatter leaves over its nest, as is its wont. The shaggy and corrugated bark of the old trees is larvæ-haunted, and consequently mouse-like creepers abound. These little creatures on every trunk showed conspicuously as they ran their marvellous adaptation to an end, and fulfilled it perfectly. All the wood-birds were there—the Whitethroat, the Wood and the Willow Wren, the Chiffchaff, and Garden-warbler. These sang from the leafy boughs. But higher up, towards the escarpment, the floor of the wood was rugged and rock-strewn. Boulders had rolled from above, and among these dwelt weasels and ermines. There were at least a pair of martins, and foxes from the fells had their tracks through the woods. A primitive mansion had once stood in the wood, but now was gone. It had been large, and green mounds, now laid low, marked out its dimensions. Old oak-panelling, with long-gone dates, were sometimes dug up, and these were covered with carvings—"carvings quaint and curious, all made out of the carver's brain." Lying around this had been an extensive orchard, the rich, though old trees of which remained. And now, in this glorious summer-time, the golden fruit fell unheeded to the ground. For Hazelhurst was long distant from town or nearest village. Brambles held their luscious fruit, and every species of ground berry grew there. No wonder it was a paradise to mice and squirrels and birds. They revelled in nature's ample provision, and were undisturbed.

Here, in the days of our immediate ancestors, Badgers were plentiful. Now, where a ridge of rock ran through the wood, there was a hole, the entrance to a somewhat spacious cavity. This could be seen for the seeking, not otherwise. Brambles and ground-ivy protected it. Black bryony and woodbine twisted up every available stem, and a knot of blackthorn grew over all. The spot was protected and dense. One day we invaded it, but after long crawling and sticking fast had to return. In it lived the badgers—had done so time out of mind, and the few poachers who knew it called it "Brockholes." "Brock" is the old north-country word for badger, and, as we have said, everything testified to its presence. In this wild fruit paradise at least two pairs of badgers bred. Each pair had more than one apartment—at least the young were not produced in that which formed the general abode. These were at the ends of the burrow, where were the beds, composed of roots and dried grass. The young were brought forth in April, and after about six weeks might have been seen sitting about the mouth of their hole, or accompanying their dam to short distances when on her evening rambles. We always found the badgers unoffending, harmless creatures unless first attacked. They fed almost entirely on roots, wild fruit, grain, and occasionally insects. They were, however, extremely shy and wary. Beautiful it was to see these creatures on summer evenings searching for food among the low bushes, occasionally giving a low grunt when some favourite root was turned up. When insects came within their reach they were snapped up somewhat after the manner of a dog catching flies. The life of the badger is eminently that of a peaceful creature, harmless in all its ways, unoffending, interesting in its life-history, useful, and, above all, fitted with a quiet contentment almost human. The body of the badger is long and heavy and its legs short, which give it an awkward shambling appearance when running. Its beautifully-shaped head has two long lines running from the snout to the tips of the ears. The upper parts of its body are light grey, becoming darker below, the lower parts being quite black.

The total length of a fully-grown male badger

is about thirty-six inches. The structure of the creature is especially adapted to its mode of life, this being shown in the slender muzzle, with movable snout, which is employed in digging. It is when thus occupied, too, that the short, stout limbs are seen fulfilling their end; and when no natural cavity exists it is these limbs and snout that provide one. Both are brought into frequent requisition when digging for roots, of certain of which the badger is particularly fond. Badgers are quite susceptible of domestication, and a friend had a pair which he led about in collars. They are possessed of great affection for their young, and rush blindly into danger, or even suffer themselves to be killed, in attempting to rescue them. . . . .

We have stretched our length along a slab of rock which margins the bank and recedes far under it. The stream for the most part is rapid, but here narrows to slow, black depth. Ever and ceaselessly does the water chafe and lap among the shelving rocks, and this, with the constant "drip," only seems to make the silence audible. Fungi and golden mosses light up our dark retreat. Never was green more green nor lichen tracery more ravishing. Close-clinging and rock-loving is all life here. Water percolates through the bank, and spreads its silver filament over all. Far out and beyond the deep wood it comes from the scaurs, and the limestone sends its carbonate to dome our retreat. Miniature stalactites hang from the roof, and bright bosses rise from the floor. Frail fern fronds depend from the crevices, and as the light rushes in, masses of golden saxifrage gild all the chamber. The beams will not long stay, for the sun dips in the western woods. From the mouth of our recess we take in a silent river reach. It is thickly embowered and overhung. Long drooping racemes of green tree flowers attract innumerable insects, especially those of the lime, and intent upon these a flycatcher sits lengthwise upon a branch. How beautiful are its short flights, the iridescence of its plumage, its white eye-lines, and barred forehead! Numerous small waterfalls, the gauze and film veils of which, when the wind blows, and dripping moss, have attracted the dippers. Kingfishers, too, in their green flight, dash over the still water. The remote pines have lost their light, and stand black against the sky. Sundown has come, and it is the hour of vesper hymns. The woods are loud swelling volumes of sound. Behind us is a woodland enchanted, though with no sadder spirits than blackbirds and thrushes that whistle to cheer it. This loud evening hymn lasts for an hour, then subsides, and the woods hush. The stem of the silver birch ceases to vibrate to the blackbird's whistle. The polyglot woodthrush is dreaming of gilded fly and dewy morn, and finally that last far-off song has ceased. Silence — an intense holy calm — is over the woods. Chill comes, the dew rises, and twilight; — and the night side of nature. How rich and varied is that of the stream side! The fern-owls with their soft plumage and noiseless flight come out, as do the great moths and bustards.

This prevalence of life at the same time is as Nature would have it—the one acting as food for the other. The beat of unseen pinions is heard above, but no object visible—some night-haunting bird flying off to its feeding ground. Through the short night summer snipe whistle and wail. Newly-arrived crakes call from the meadows, and a disturbed lapwing gets up crying from the green cornstalks. Maybe the disturber was the hare whose almost human cry now comes from the thorn fence. For it the corn sprouts have come for the last time, and soon it will be in the poacher's wallet. A loud splash comes from the water, and a great black trout has sucked down its prey. This is a large-winged night-fly. That first splash is a token of more abundant night food, and soon the reach boils. Every speckled trout is "on its feed." How we long for the pliant, sympathetic rod! Then, ye lusty trout, how would the undefinable thrill rush at intervals up our arm! But our mission to-night is not this. The herons scream, the wood-owls hoot, and—what is that other night sound? The crescent moon shows a bit of light at intervals; soon masses of cloud intervene.

A faint whistle, unlike that of any bird, comes up stream, and although imperceptible the dark, still water is moved. The trout cease to rise. The whistle comes nearer, and then a rustle is heard. The osier beds are stirred, and some long dark object makes its way between the parted stems. A movement would dispel the dark shadow, and which in turn would divide the dark water and take it silently away. The otters have reconnoitered, and all is safe. They come paddling down stream, and, arriving at the pool, stop, tumble and frolic, rolling over and over, and round and round, and performing the most marvellous evolutions you could possibly conceive. They swing on the willow spray, and dash with lightning velocity at a piece of floating bark, tumble with it, wrestle with it, and go through a hundred wonderful movements. They are motionless, then begin to play, and so continue for nearly an hour, when, as if suddenly alarmed, they rush down stream to their fishing grounds, and leave us cold and benumbed. We plod through the meadow beneath the moon and stars, chilled to the marrow by the falling dew.

Otters are still abundant on the banks of most

northern streams, as also among the rocks and boulders of the coast-line. Human invasion drives them from their haunts, although, where waters remain unpolluted, they not unfrequently pass up the rivers by towns and villages during the still night. On the margins of the more secluded tarns of the fells, otters, too, are yet found. Fitted for an aquatic existence, the structure of the otter beautifully exhibits the provisions suitable to its mode of life. On land it can travel swiftly, though the water is its best element. Immersed in this, its coat appears smooth and glossy. In pursuing its prey it performs the most graceful movements, doubling and diving so rapidly that it is difficult to follow its evolutions. When fishing, its object is to get beneath the object pursued, as, from the construction of its eyes, which are placed high in the head, it is better enabled to secure its prey. This it seldom fails to do, its whole structure, as already remarked, greatly facilitating its movements in the water. Its uniform dusky brown coat has, like all aquatic creatures, a soft under-fur with long hair above.

The otter generally takes possession of a natural cavity, a drain, or a hole made by the inundation of the stream. The entrance is usually under water, and inclines towards the bank. Situations where the latter is overhung with bushes and with tall water plants in the vicinity are generally chosen. From this the young, when three or four weeks old, betake themselves to the water. If captured now they may easily be domesticated. One of our friends has to-day a young otter, which he leads about in a leash. At Bassenthwaite a man and his son trained a pair of otters to fish in the lake. They would return when called upon, or follow their master home when the fishing was over. The males in spring fight desperately, and once, when hidden, we witnessed a fight which lasted an hour, and so engrossed did the combatants become that we approached and, taking the part of the lesser, shot its aggressor.

And now a word as to the food of the otter. That it destroys fish we are not about to deny. But this liking for fish has become such a stereotyped fact (?) in natural history that it is glibly repeated, parrot-like, and so continues until most readers have come to accept it. The otter destroys but few fish, using the word in its popular acceptation. What it destroys are for food, and not out of love of killing. The greater part of its diet consists of fresh-water crayfish, thousands of which it destroys, and it is for these that long journeys are so frequently made. This does not apply to the pairing season; the wanderings have then another end. Many miles in a night are traversed for these crustaceans, the beds of mountain and moorland streams being tracked to their source, almost every stone on the way being examined. At least upon two occasions have we found the remains of the moor-hen after an otter's meal.

CHAPTER IV.

COURIERS OF THE AIR.

THE power of flight being almost exclusively the characteristic attribute of birds, it is somewhat strange that even the most eminent naturalists should be silent upon it. And yet this is almost universally so. Those who mention the speed of flight do so upon the most insufficient evidence, as witness Michelet's statement that the swallow flies at the rate of eighty leagues an hour. Roughly this gives us a thousand miles in four hours; but assuredly, even in its dashes, the swallow does not attain to anything like this speed. The Duke of Argyll is rather under than over the mark when he computes the speed at more than a hundred miles an hour. Here, however, the mechanism of flight in the swallows is carried through an ascending scale, until in the swift it reaches its highest degree of power both in endurance and facility of evolution. Although there are birds which may, and probably do, attain to a speed of one hundred and fifty miles an hour, this remarkable rate is not to be looked for in any of the birds of the swallow kind. There is something fascinating in the idea of eliminating time and space, and with this attribute popular fancy has in some measure clothed the swallows. At the greater rate of speed indicated above the swallow might, as has been stated, breakfast round the Barbican, and take its mid-day *siesta* in Algiers. This, however, is a popular myth. In their migrations swallows stick close to land, and never leave it unless compelled; they cross straits at the narrowest part, and are among the most fatiguable of birds. From this it will be seen that although swallows may possess considerable speed, they have no great powers of sustained flight or endurance. These attributes belong, in the most marked degree, to several ocean birds.

Any one who has crossed the Atlantic must have noticed that gulls accompany the ship over the whole distance; or, at least, are never absent throughout the voyage. The snowy "sea swallows," as the terns are called, seem quite tireless on the wing; though the petrels and albatross alone deserve the name of oceanic birds. Sir Edwin Arnold, in an account of his voyage to America, writes as follows of the sea-swallows: " Every day we see playing round the ship and skimming up and down the wave-hollows companies of lovely little terns and sea-swallows, the latter no larger than thrushes. These fearless people of the waste have not by any means followed us from land, living, as gulls often will, on the waste thrown from the vessel. They are vague and casual roamers of the ocean, who spying the great steamship from afar, have sailed close up, to see if we are a rock or an island, and will then skim away on their own free and boundless business. Yonder tiny bird with purple and green plumage, his little breast and neck laced with silver, is distant one thousand miles at this moment from a drop of fresh water, and yet cares no more for the fact than did the Irish squire who 'lived twelve miles from a lemon.' If his wings ever grow weary it is but to settle quietly on the bosom of a great billow and suffer it for a time to rock and roll him amid this hissing spendrift, the milky flying foam, and the broken sea-lace which forms and gleams and disappears again upon the dark slopes. When he pleases, a stroke of the small red foot and a beat of the wonderful wing launch him off from the jagged edge of his billow, and he flits past us at one hundred knots an hour, laughing steam and canvas to scorn, and steering for some nameless crag in Labrador or Fundy, or bound, it may be, homeward for some island or marsh of the far-away Irish coast. Marvellously expressive of power as is our untiring engine, which all day and all night throbs and pants and pulses in noisy rhythm under the deck, what a clumsy affair it is compared to the dainty plumes and delicate muscles which carry that pretty, fearless sea-swallow back to his roost."

No deserts seem to bound the range of the petrels, and they are found at every distance from land. Different species inhabit every ocean — from the fulmar in the far north to the giant petrel which extends its flight to the icebanks of the south. Here the Antarctic and snowy petrels appear, floating upon the drift ice, and never leaving these dreary seas. Another bird of immense wing power is the tiny stormy petrel, the smallest web-footed bird known. It belongs to every sea, and although so seeming frail it breasts the utmost fury of the storm, skimming with incredible velocity the trough of the waves, and gliding rapidly over their snowy crests. Petrels have been observed two thousand miles from nearest land, whilst at half that distance Sir James Ross once saw a couple of penguins quietly paddling in the sea. A pair of the rudimentary wings of this bird are lying before me as I write. These are simply featherless paddles, but by their aid so rapidly does the bird swim that it almost defies many of the fishes to equal it. The enormous appetite of the giant penguin (which weighs about eighty pounds) may have something to do with its restricted powers of flight, and in the stomach of one of these Ross found ten pounds of quartz, granite, and trap fragments, swallowed most likely to promote digestion.

But surely the lord of the winged race is the bird which does not rest; and this may almost be said of the man-of-war or frigate bird. He is a navigator who never reaches his bourne, and from his almost ceaseless flight it would seem as though earth and sea were equally prohibited to him. To a bird with such an immense and superior wing apparatus, the metaphor, "he sleeps upon the storm," becomes almost literal. This black, solitary bird is nearly nothing more than wings, his prodigious pinions measuring fifteen feet, even surpassing those of the condor of the Andes. Although sometimes seen four hundred leagues from land, the frigate bird is said to return every night to its solitary roost.

Of all birds, the albatross has, perhaps, the most extended powers of flight. It has been known to follow a vessel for several successive days without once touching the water except to pick up floating food; and even then it does not rest. In describing the flight of this bird from personal observation, Captain Hutton writes as follows: "The flight of the albatross is truly majestic, as with outstretched motionless wings he sails over the surface of the sea—now rising high in the air, now with a bold sweep and wings inclined at an angle with the horizon, descending until the tip of the lower one all but touches the crests of the waves as he skims over them. I have sometimes watched narrowly one of these birds sailing and wheeling about in all directions for more than an hour without seeing the slightest movement of the wings, and have never witnessed anything to equal the ease and grace of this bird as he sweeps past, often within a few yards—every part of his body perfectly motionless except the head and eye, which turn slowly and seem to take notice of everything. 'Tranquil its spirit seemed and floated slow; even in its very motion there was rest.'" But these birds and the frigate bird are sea and ocean species, and, with rare exceptions, are able to rest upon the waters. This, however, cannot be said of many of the land birds, and here observation is easier.

As an antithesis to the apparently lifeless wings of the albatross, Pettigrew compares the ceaseless activity of those of the humming-bird. In these delicate and exquisitely beautiful birds, the wings, according to Gould, move so rapidly when the bird is poised before an object that it is impossible for the eye to follow each stroke, and a hazy circle of indistinctness on each side the bird is all that is perceptible. When a humming-bird flies in a horizontal direction, it occasionally proceeds with such velocity as altogether to elude observation. Mention of the calm majestic flight of the albatross suggests the possibility of birds resting on the wing. An American naturalist asserts that birds of prey and some others have the power to lock securely together those parts of the wing holding the extended feathers, and corresponding to the fingers of the human hand. The action of the air on the wing in this condition extends the elbow, which is prevented from opening too far by a cartilage, and the wings may keep this position for an indefinite length of time, with no muscular action whatever on the part of the bird. While resting in this way, the bird cannot rise in a still atmosphere; but if there be a horizontal current, it may allow itself to be carried along by it, with a slight tendency downward, and so gain a momentum by which, with a slight change of direction, it may rise to some extent, still without muscular action of the wings. This same naturalist also believes it quite possible for birds to sleep on the wing. As bearing on this subject, Professor J. S. Newbury asserts that he once shot a bird which came slowly to the ground as if still flying, but reached it dead. He believed that it had died high in the air; but had never been able to account for the manner of its descent till now, when he found an explanation in the statement just given.

Thousands of gold-crests annually cross and recross the North Sea at the wildest periods of the year, and unless the weather is rough generally make their migrations in safety. And yet this is the smallest and frailest British bird— a mere fluff of feathers, weighing only seventy grains. Another of the tits, the oxeye, has been met upon two occasions at six hundred and nine hundred miles from land. With regard to those birds which cross the Atlantic, it matters not for our purpose whether they are driven by stress of weather or cross voluntarily—suffice it they come. Less likely birds that have occurred in Britain are the belted kingfisher and American yellow-billed cuckoo. The white-winged crossbill must be mentioned with less certainty, for, although a North American bird, it is also found in some northern European countries.

All birds of great and sustained powers of flight have one well-marked characteristic—they have long wings, with sharply-pointed ends. The general truth of this will be at once admitted if the rule be applied to the various species mentioned above. Another point is worthy of notice. The apparent speed of flight to an unpractised eye is most deceptive. A heron, as it rises and flaps languidly along the course of a brook, appears not only to progress slowly but to use its wings in like manner. Yet the Duke of Argyll has pointed out, and any one may verify the statement by his watch, that the heron seldom flaps his wings at a rate of less than from one hundred and twenty to one hundred and fifty times in a minute. This is counting only the downward strokes, so that the bird really makes from two hundred and forty to three hundred separate movements a minute. The rook and heron fly in almost straight lines, have large rounded wings, and float with the greatest ease upon the air. The rook in its measured flight makes about five-and-twenty miles an hour; the heron thirty. Our short-winged game birds fly with incredible velocity, and any attempt to observe or count their wing movements leaves but a blurred impression on the eye, whilst in some species so quick is the vibratory movement as to prevent its being seen. Driven grouse flying "down wind" have been known to seriously stun sportsmen by falling upon their heads. A grouse does not move its wings so rapidly as a partridge, though the late C. S. was once clean knocked out of a battery by a grouse he had shot falling upon him; and in this way loaded guns have frequently been fired by dead birds. The Duke of Beaufort upon one occasion picked up a brace of grouse which had cannoned and killed each other in mid-air, and colliding is not an unfrequent occurrence. As illustrating a remarkable quality of flight, the case of the kestrel or windhover may be taken. On a summer day one may frequently see this pretty little falcon standing against the blue in what seems an absolutely stationary position, as though suspended by an invisible silken thread. But let a meadow-mouse so much as move and it drops to the sward in an instant.

As has been already stated, there is perhaps nothing more wonderful in nature than the power of flight, and no subject which yields such startling facts upon investigation. "The way of an eagle in the air" is one of those things of which Solomon expressed himself ignorant; and there is something truly marvellous in the mechanism which controls the scythe-like sweep of wings peculiar to most birds of prey. The noblest of these, the peregrine, has been seen flying over mid-Atlantic; and Henry IV., King of France, had a falcon which escaped from Fontainebleau, and in twenty-four hours after was found in Malta, a space computed to be not less than 1,350 miles, a velocity equal to fifty-six miles an hour, supposing the hawk to have been on the wing the whole time. Indeed, in Montagu's opinion, the rapidity with which hawks and other birds occasionally fly is probably not less than at the rate of a hundred and fifty miles an hour, when either pursued or pursuing. The speed of flight of the peregrine cited above is about that of our best trained pigeons; and it may here be remarked that the flight of these two (otherwise dissimilar) birds very much resembles each other. The beautiful swallow-tailed kite has accomplished the feat of flying across the whole Atlantic Ocean, which is hardly to be wondered at seeing its vast powers of flight. Lieuwenholk relates an exciting chase which he saw in a menagerie about one hundred feet long between a swallow and a dragon-fly (Mordella). The insect flew with incredible speed, and wheeled with such address that the swallow, notwithstanding its utmost efforts, completely failed to overtake and capture it. The best speed of a railway train is only a little more than half the velocity of the golden eagle, the flight of which often attains to the rate of one hundred and forty miles an hour. Of all birds, the condor mounts highest into the atmosphere. Humboldt describes the flight of this bird in the Andes to be at least twenty thousand feet above the level of the sea. Upon one occasion a falcon was observed to cut a snipe right in two, with such strength and speed did it cut down its prey. Sparrow-hawks and merlins have not unfrequently been known to crash through thick plate-glass windows when in pursuit of prey, or at caged birds.

Of all British birds, none is so beautiful or so secluded in its habits as the kingfisher. Its presence is peculiarly in keeping with the rapid rocky trout streams which it loves to haunt. Its low, arrow-like flight, as it darts like a streak of azure, green, and gold, is familiar to every angler. He hears it far down stream; it comes under the old ivied bridge, passes like a flash, and is gone—how quickly the following will show. Mr. George Rooper, the well-known Biographer of the Salmon, was travelling on the Great Western Railway, which between Pangbourne and Reading runs parallel with, and close to, the Thames. As the train approached the river a kingfisher started from the bank and flew along the river for nearly a mile. Mr. Rooper watched it the whole distance, and its relative position with the window never varied a yard; the bird flying at exactly the same pace as that at which the train travelled, and which the observer had just previously ascertained to be fifty-five miles an hour. This is about half the speed at which the eider-duck flies, as, when fairly on the wing, it makes upwards of one hundred and twenty miles an hour. The rapidity with which all birds of the plover kind fly is well known, and a "trip" of golden plover have been seen midway between Hawaii and the mainland. An officer in Donald Currie's line recently brought home with him a specimen of the St. Helena waxbill which he caught when on watch on the bridge of the *Grantully Castle*. At the time the nearest land was distant a thousand miles, and the little captive was so distressed that it quietly allowed the officer to capture it.

It has been computed that a red-throated diver swims about four and a half miles on the surface of the water, and between six and seven beneath the surface per hour. Macgillivray states that upon one occasion he watched a flock of red-breasted mergansers pursuing sand eels, when the birds seemed to move under the water with almost as much velocity as in the air, and often rose to breathe at a distance of two hundred yards from the spot at which they had dived. To show to what depth this bird flies beneath the water it may be mentioned that one was caught in a net at thirty fathoms; while a shag, or green cormorant, has been caught in a crab pot fixed at twenty fathoms below the surface; and guillemots literally fly under water without even using their feet. As bearing directly on the interesting subject of flight under water the case of another of the divers may be mentioned. It has been said that one of the strong and original strokes of nature was when she made the "loon," a bird which represents the wildness and solitariness of the wildest and most solitary spots. It dives with such marvellous quickness that the shot of the gunner gets there just in time to cut across a circle of descending tail feathers and a couple of little jets of water flung upward by the web feet of the loon. Speaking of this bird Burroughs says that in the water "its wings are more than wings. It plunges into this denser air, and flies with incredible speed. Its head and beak form a sharp point to its tapering neck. Its wings are far in front, and its legs equally far in the rear, and its course through the crystal depths is like the speed of an arrow. In the northern lakes it has been taken forty feet under water upon hooks baited for the great lake trout. I had never seen one till last fall, when one appeared on the river in front of my house. I knew instantly it was the loon. Who could not tell a loon a half-mile or more away, though he had never seen one before? The river was like glass, and every movement of the bird as it sported about broke the surface into ripples, that revealed it far and wide. Presently a boat shot out from shore, and went ripping up the surface toward the loon. The creature at once seemed to divine the intentions of the boatman, and sidled off obliquely, keeping a sharp look-out as if to make sure it was pursued. A steamer came down and passed between them, and when the way was again clear the loon was still swimming on the surface. Presently it disappeared under the water, and the boatman pulled sharp and hard. In a few moments the bird reappeared some rods further on, as if to make an observation. Seeing it was being pursued, and no mistake, it dived quickly, and when it came up again had gone many times as far as the boat had in the same space of time. Then it dived again, and distanced its pursuer so easily that he gave over the chase and rested upon his oars. But the bird made a final plunge, and when it emerged upon the surface again it was over a mile away. Its course must have been, and doubtless was, an actual flight under water, and half as fast as the crow flies in the air. The loon would have delighted the old poets. Its wild, demoniac laughter awakens the echoes on the solitary lakes, and its ferity and hardiness were kindred to those robust spirits." Another specially interesting bird which does something nearly approaching to flying under water is the dipper. The ouzel is essentially a bird of the running brook, though as to what part this pretty white-breasted thrush plays in the economy of nature naturalists are by no means agreed. Its most frequent stand is upon some mossy stone in a river reach, and here its crescented form may oftenest be seen. It haunts the brightly-running streams in winter as in summer, and when these are transformed into roaring torrents seems to love them best. Let us watch it awhile. It dashes through the spray and into the white foam, performing its morning ablutions. Then it emerges to perch on a stone, always jerking its body about, and dipping, dipping, ever dipping. Presently it melts into the water like a bubble, but immediately emerges to regain its seat, then trills out a loud wren-like song, but, breaking off short, again disappears. We are standing on an old stone bridge, and are enabled to observe it closely. By a rapid, vibratory motion of the wings, it drives itself down through the water, and by the aid of its wide-spreading feet clings to and walks among the pebbles. These it rapidly turns over with its bill, searching for the larvæ of water flies and gauzy-winged *ephemeræ*. It searches the brook carefully downwards, sometimes clean immersed, at other times with its back out, then with the water barely covering its feet. It does not always work with the stream, as we have frequently seen him struggling against it, but retaining its position upon the bottom. Even at the present day there are naturalists who, from the examination of cabinet specimens, aver that it is not in the power of the bird to walk on the bottom of the brook, but then they know nothing of him along his native streams.

Taking advantage of two birds remarkable for their long and sustained powers of flight, experiments have recently been conducted with a view to utilising swallows and pigeons as war messengers. In this connection the use of trained pigeons is one of the oldest institutions in the world; though now that certain European Powers have trained falcons to cut down pigeons, it is said that the pigeon-post is not sufficiently reliable. In consequence a number of French *savants* recently approached the Minister of War, and induced him to found a military swallow-cote whence the birds might be trained. The Governor of Lille was charged to test the plan, and certain experiments made at Roubaix last year are now commanded to be repeated under the supervision of Captain Degouy of the Engineers. During the coming autumn this gentleman is to be present at a grand flight of messenger swallows; and if his report is favourable, a swallow-cote will be founded and placed under the care of special trainers at Mont Valérian. The idea of engaging swallows in war is a pretty one, as in future all European wars will have to be conducted in "Swallow-time"—when the warm winds blow from the sunny south. This arrangement will at least obviate night-watches in frozen trenches; nor is it likely that pickets will any longer be starved to death at their posts. The incident is also quoted in proof of the fact that we are nearing the time when Europe will be governed by the Parliament of Man, the Federation of the World. But, after all, the idiosyncrasies of France have a way of not being fulfilled; and the reign of the swallow will doubtless be as ephemeral as that of the *brav' Général* himself. In all their military operations of late the French have made considerable use of pigeons in conveying despatches; and in the

Franco-German war the birds played a conspicuous part. Upon several occasions, indeed, the inhabitants of beleaguered cities looked upon the successful flights of these birds as their only hope betwixt death and starvation.

At the time the French were making trials with messenger swallows, the young German Emperor ordered extensive experiments to be carried out with carrier pigeons, the same to be tested at the Imperial manœuvres. Upon this, six of the first Columbarian Societies of Germany each offered to supply twenty-four birds, which are now in training. So we have it that the French are endeavouring to train swallows, the Germans pigeons, and the Russians falcons. Whether the falcons are themselves to convey messages, or are to be used to cut down the swallows and pigeons whilst so engaged, is not stated. The pigeon is a tried messenger, and has, moreover, some interesting and remarkable records. The claim of the swallow, on the other hand, lies all in its possibilities. In this connection " swallow " must stand in a generic sense, and include all birds of the swallow kind as well as the swift. Although, as already stated, swallows are among the most fatiguable of birds, yet one of the American species—the purple martin—would seem to be an exception, and the fact of its having crossed the Atlantic is well known. It is true that swallows attain to an immense speed in their rushes, and there is a well-authenticated instance of one having flown twenty miles in thirteen minutes. The probable speed of the swallow, flying straight and swift, is about one hundred and twenty miles an hour; its ordinary speed ninety miles. The swift attains to two hundred miles, and seems quite tireless on the wing. If swifts can be inspired with a sense of discipline; if French wars can invariably be arranged for the summer months; and if some arrangement can be made with the insect hosts to keep the upper air—*then* something may come of the Lille experiments. If these things cannot be, the French sharpshooter will never be asked to try flying shots at swifts rushing through the air at the rate of two hundred miles an hour. If the Russians are training falcons to catch pigeons, the Germans must train raptors to catch swallows. Here is a fact which proves the possibility. The hobby falcon, a summer migrant to Britain, hawks for dragon-flies—among the swiftest of insects—which it seizes with its foot and devours in mid-air. It cuts down swifts, larks, pigeons, and, where they are found, bee-birds—all remarkable for their great powers of flight. By way of testing the speed of flight in birds of the swallow kind, Spallanzani captured and marked a sand-martin or bank-swallow—the feeblest of its genus —on her nest at Pavia and set her free at Milan, fifteen miles away. She flew back in thirteen minutes. In striking contrast with the rate at which birds with long pointed wings fly is the fact that one of a pair of starlings (which are short-winged birds) was captured and sent in a basket a distance of upwards of thirty miles by train. It was then freed, and was three hours before it found its way back to its nestlings.

To turn from swallows to pigeons. The power of pigeons on the wing is proverbial. All trained birds of this species have two qualifications in a marked degree. The first is speed; the second long and sustained powers of flight. This proposition can be amply demonstrated, and the following are some of the most remarkable records. On the 6th of October, 1850, Sir John Ross despatched a pair of young pigeons from Assistance Bay, a little west of Wellington Sound; and on October 13th a pigeon made its appearance at the dovecote in Ayrshire, Scotland, whence Sir John had the pair he took out. The distance direct between the two places is two thousand miles. An instance is on record of a pigeon flying twenty-three miles in eleven minutes; and another flew from Rouen to Ghent, one hundred and fifty miles, in an hour and a half. An interesting incident of flight is the case of a pigeon which, in 1845, fell wounded and exhausted at Vauxhall Station, then the terminus of the South-Western Railway. It bore a message to the effect that it was one of three despatched to the Duke of Wellington from Ichaboe Island, two thousand miles away. The message was immediately sent on to his Grace, and by him acknowledged. In a pigeon competition some years ago, the winning bird flew from Ventnor to Manchester, two hundred and eight miles, at the rate of fifty-five miles an hour. As an experiment a trained pigeon was recently dispatched from a northern newspaper office with a request that it might be liberated for its return journey at 9.45 a.m. It reached home at 1.10 p.m. having covered in the meantime one hundred and forty miles, flying at the rate of forty miles an hour. In the north pigeons have long been used to convey messages between country houses and market towns; and in Russia they are now being employed to convey negatives of photographs taken in balloons. The first experiment of the kind was made from the cupola of the Cathedral of Isaac, and the subject photographed was the Winter Palace. The plates were packed in envelopes impenetrable to light, and then tied to the feet of the pigeons, which safely and quickly carried them to the station at Volkovo. Here is another interesting instance of speed and staying power. The pigeons in this case flew from Bordeaux to Manchester, and not only beat all existing records, but flew more than seventy miles further than anything previousiy attempted by English flyers. The winning bird flew at the rate of eighteen hundred and seventy-nine yards a minute, or over sixty-four miles an hour, and that for a distance of one hundred and forty-two and a half miles. The same club has flown birds distances of six hundred and thirteen, and six hundred and twenty-five miles. These latter, however, were several days in returning, and in their case the only wonder is that they could accomplish the distance at all. The following is still more interesting, as it entailed a race between birds and insects. A pigeon-fancier of Hamme, in Westphalia, made a wager that a dozen bees liberated three miles from their hive would reach it in better time than a dozen pigeons would reach their cot from the same distance. The competitors were given wing at Rhynhern, a village nearly a league from Hamme, and the first bee finished a quarter of a minute in advance of the first pigeon, three other bees reached the goal before the second pigeon, the main body of both detachments finishing almost simultaneously an instant or two later. The bees, too, may be said to have been handicapped in the race, having been rolled in flour before starting for purposes of identification.

The American passenger pigeon compasses the whole Atlantic ocean. The speed of its flight is approximately known; it is able to

F

cover one thousand six hundred miles in twenty-four hours. This, however, is marvellous, when it is seen that, flying at the rate of nearly seventy miles an hour, it takes the bird two days and nights to cross. What must be the nature of the mechanism that can stand such a strain as this? This pigeon is now recognised as a British bird. Several examples have occurred, and whilst some of these were probably "escapes," others doubtless were wild birds. These had perfect plumage, were taken in an exhausted condition, and their crops showed only the slightest traces of food. As is well known, the passenger pigeon is a bird of immense powers of flight, and in its overland journeys often flies at the rate of a mile a minute. Wild birds, however, can only come from America; and this opens up the interesting question as to the possibility of birds crossing the Atlantic without once resting. Naturalists of the present day say that this feat is not only probable, but that it is accomplished by several birds. Mr. Darwin somewhere asserts that one or two of them are annually blown across the ocean; and it is certain that half-a-dozen species have occurred upon the west coasts of England and Ireland, which are found nowhere but in North America. Mr. Howard Saunders states that passenger pigeons are often captured in the State of New York with their crops still filled with the undigested grains of rice that must have been taken in the distant fields of Georgia and South Carolina; apparently proving that they passed over the intervening space within a few hours. It certainly seems remarkable that a bird should have the power of winging its way over four thousand miles of sea; but recently two persons have recorded the fact that they have noticed pigeons settle upon the water to drink, then rise from it with apparent ease. And Mr. Darwin says that, where the banks of the Nile are perpendicular, whole flocks of pigeons have been seen to settle on the water and drink while they floated down the stream. He adds that, seen from a distance, they resemble flocks of gulls on the surface of the sea. The passenger pigeon is one of the handsomest of its kind. The accounts of its migrations in search of food are known to all. It is said to move in such vast flocks as to darken the earth as they pass over, and that one of these columns brings devastation wherever it comes.

In the Anglo-Belgian pigeon races, some of the birds attain to nearly a mile a minute, and this when the race is for five hundred miles. The English, French, and Germans all rear pigeons in their fortresses; and the birds are utilised by the Trinity House in conveying messages from the lightships. They are also in use on the Indian stations. The following are additional remarkable instances of quick and long sustained powers of flight which show what the pigeon is capable of doing. Thirty-three birds were recently brought from Termonde, in Belgium, and were liberated at Sunderland at 5 a.m. A telegram received at the latter place stated that sixteen of the birds reached home at 1.35 the same afternoon, having accomplished the distance of four hundred and eighty miles in about eight and a half hours, or about fifty-six miles an hour. A week previous the same birds had flown from London to Brussels.

It has frequently been suggested that homing pigeons should be used to carry telegraphic messages between country houses and post offices. In many cases pigeons have been used as telegraphic messengers with the most successful results. Sending into town, by the people of the Hall is a frequent occurrence, and whenever a messenger had occasion to go, some pigeons, bred at the Hall are sent in a hamper by the dog-cart or what-not. These are taken possession of by a local tradesman living near the post office, who also receives the telegrams. The latter are rolled up and tied either round the bird's leg, or so that it lies across the upper part of its breast. The pigeon is then liberated, and in about ten minutes from the time of despatch the telegram is delivered at the Hall, five miles distant. The reverse process is repeated with the tradesman's pigeons kept at the Hall if a reply to the telegram is required. The platform leading into the pigeon-house is connected with an electric bell that rings when the pigeon, reaching home, alights on the platform, and thus notifies the servants the arrival of a telegram; one of them then goes and unties it from the bird's neck. Much saving in porterage is thus accomplished; the telegrams are delivered in a few minutes, and rarely, if ever, lost. The ordinary homing pigeon is best adapted for the purpose, being an inexpensive purchase. In proof of this fitness the following most remarkable incident may be recorded. A number of English homers were recently sent to Lassay, an inland town of France, but for some reason the French police authorities refused to start them, and the birds were relegated to Cherbourg, where they were liberated at 7 a.m. One of them was seen to alight on the roof of its loft at 11.30 the same forenoon. It had accomplished the entire distance of about three hundred miles, including one hundred miles of water, in a bee-line from Cherbourg to Birkenhead at the rate of over a mile a minute. This particular bird had never been any great distance from home, and although English bred it was from a famous strain of Belgian "homers." The large provincial towns in the north of England are the great centres of pigeon-flying. Recently as many as two thousand five hundred birds were liberated at a flight. Every one of these pigeons were out of sight in one minute from the time they were thrown up, a fact which shows how strong is the "homing" instinct within them. The homing pigeon may not supersede the telegraph; but in disturbed times it is the business of an enemy to cut the wires, to tap them, or even to send misleading despatches along them. No such danger need be apprehended from a carrier pigeon, for, if well trained, it will fly straight from loft to loft, never parting with its tiny scroll unless killed or taken—a mishap which is not likely to befall more than one or two of a flight. As already stated, some remarkable results have already been achieved, not only by Government birds—whose performances and proceedings are, of course, kept secret—but by those belonging to the numerous carrier-pigeon societies which have been established on the Continent either for mere amusement or with more patriotic objects in view. Thus, some years ago, a homing pigeon covered the six hundred and fifteen miles —air-line—between Liége, in Belgium, and San Sebastian, in Spain, in the course of a single day; and in the United States as much as five hundred miles has been traversed in from twenty-four to twenty-eight hours—that is, the birds were absent from loft to loft for that period. But, as the progress of the pigeon from one station to another cannot be accurately followed, it may have halted on the way. The bird is believed to travel the first day without stopping, and being stiff and sore, to rest the second day, resuming its journey on the third, since it is seldom that "a return" comes back travel-stained or weary.

When the rearing and training of carrier-pigeons for French military service was seriously undertaken, the first thing to be done was to find a breed of birds at once intelligent, hardy, strong, light on the wing, and of a dull, uniform colour, likely to escape notice and pursuit. All these attributes are possessed by the Belgian breed, which is divided into two classes; the large, heavy Antwerp, and the smaller, lighter Luttrich variety. The scientific training, which must be begun early, is as follows: As soon as the young pigeons can fly they are taken out of the pigeon-house, put into a basket, and carried (always with the flying-hole of the basket kept carefully turned towards the pigeon-house), to an unknown spot at a short distance, where they are set free and let fly home. It is seldom that a pigeon fails, in the first short trial, to find its way back to its paternal nest. At each trial the distance is slightly lengthened. Pigeons six months old are liberated at a distance of eighty kilometres from home, those of a year old at one hundred and fifty kilometres, those of two years at three hundred kilometres, and older tried birds at six hundred to eight hundred kilometres. These, of course, are average measurements, and are varied according to circumstance. The percentage of losses naturally increases with increasing distance. In long flights the birds meet with innumerable hindrances; rain, hail, fog, wind, and thunderstorms not only impede their flight, but often affect their wonderful sense of locality and direction. The birds are remarkably sensitive to electricity, so that thunderstorms are peculiarly baffling to them, and large forests, great extents of water, and ranges of mountains influence and alter the upper air currents, by the direction of which the pigeons, taught by some marvellous "instinct," are able to steer their course. The average speed of a pigeon is reckoned at a kilometre a minute, and on this basis, and taking into consideration the time of year, length of daylight, weather, &c., calculations are made of the distance a pigeon can be sent. In summer, when daylight begins at half-past three in the morning and lasts till half-past eight at night, a trained pigeon can fly about one thousand kilometres in a day, while on a foggy November day, when the daylight begins late and darkness comes on early, the same bird cannot accomplish more than four hundred kilometres. One great drawback hitherto attendant on the use of pigeons has been the supposed impossibility of making them fly backwards and forwards between two points; they would only fly in one direction. Now, however, Captain Malogoli, the head of the Italian military carrier pigeon depôts, has, after immense and unwearying trouble, succeeded in getting his pigeons to fly backwards and forwards between Rome and Civita Vecchia (seventy-two kilometres). This practical success has shattered the theories of various ornithologists, as Russ, who have affirmed that pigeons cannot be made to fly in two directions. The chief points to be observed in the rearing of pigeons are—roomy, warm houses, facing toward the sun; scrupulous cleanliness, light food, and abundance of clean, fresh water. The smaller the bird, and the quieter its colour, the better chance it stands of safety from human and other enemies; among the latter the falcon is the most dangerous. The military pigeon-post is best organised in Germany, Italy, and France. In the last French budget a sum of sixty-eight thousand francs was devoted to this branch of the service, and there are at present in France twenty-two sub-depôts, besides the chief pigeon station. In Italy there are twelve sub-depôts, and five in the Italian possessions in Africa.

The following are the regulations as to training and flying in connection with the messenger war pigeons in Italy. The posts of Digdegha, the wells of Tata, as well as the detachments sent out to reconnoitre towards Ailet, Assur, &c., send their reports by means of pigeons from the dovecote installed at Massowa, whence they are forwarded to the headquarters at Saati. On rainy days, and when the communications are confidential, the despatches are introduced into goose-quills and sealed ; but as this operation, above all when the troops are on the march, entails a certain loss of time, they must only, when possible, write a despatch on a leaf of a pocket-book with which every officer and non-commissioned officer is provided ; the despatch is then tied to a tail-feather of the bird. Conventional signs are also used in the case of a detachment being surprised by the enemy and not having time to send a telegram. For instance, when one or more pigeons arrive at the dovecote without despatches, and with the loss of some tail feathers, it is a sign that the troops have been attacked. Sometimes marks made with colour supply such-and-such information. Each detachment carries three or four pigeons in a light basket of bamboo and net. The distances being short, each despatch is sent by one pigeon. A first despatch is sent at the hour fixed in advance by the commander, the others successively as there is news to transmit. The pigeon-basket is borne by soldiers, who relieve one another at stated intervals. The grains of wheat and vessels of water are confided to a corporal, who has the care of the pigeons. When the detachment has to remain absent more than a day, they take with them four pigeons, with wheat and water in a leathern case. If they have to return in a day, they carry but three pigeons, with the food and drink necessary. The frequent arrival of these birds from all quarters presents a curious appearance. When they arrive they perch at the window of the dovecot, where their mates and young await them. To enter they must pass through a sort of cage-trap, which does not permit them to return, and at the same time separates them from the other pigeons. The weight of the newcomer sets an electric bell ringing; and this signal continues all the time the bird remains in the trap; thus giving notice to the sergeant of the guard, who takes the despatch and forwards it to headquarters.

The liability of so defenceless a bird as the pigeon to attack has led to experiments being undertaken from time to time with young ravens, which make fairly quick and reliable messengers up to a distance of about fifty miles. As the raven is very teachable (it can be made to "retrieve" most creditably), and as it manifests a strong attachment to its birth-place, there seems no reason why its training should not be further extended in the new direction, for which its great spirit and endurance appear eminently to fit it.

Here I have only touched upon the speed and power of flight, but the whole subject is one of the most fascinating branches of natural history. No reference has been made to the marvellous movements of birds in the air, which constitute the very poetry of motion—the stationary balancing, hovering, circling, and gliding, all of which may be observed, especially among our own birds of prey.

Although much is known of the speed of birds and animals, there are but few ascertained facts concerning that of insects and fishes. The comparatively low intelligence of these two classes of animals makes it difficult to direct them. They rarely fly or swim in anything approaching to a straight line, and experiments give only approximate results. Pike in pursuit of their prey seem to flash through the water; and salmon and trout move almost as quickly. The Spanish mackerel, with its smooth, cone-shaped body, is among the swiftest of fishes, and for speed only finds a parallel in the dolphin. There is a great similarity in shape between these two, and both cut the water like a yatch. The first follows the fastest steamers with the greatest ease, in its dashes swimming at five times their speed. The bonito is also a fast swimmer; and all those fishes "trimmed" in like fashion with him.

There is one insect to which attention may be drawn, as affording a most striking example of speed among lowly-winged creatures. That is the dragon-fly. I have frequently had an opportunity of dropping into company with the largest species (*Libellula grandis*), in its aerial excursions in autumn by a particular roadside, along which there was a rushy-margined pool. At such times the writer has been occasionally on foot,—more frequently driving. On foot one has scarcely any means of judging of its speed, for in a moment it is past and gone out of sight. But what is the experience when you are driving, say at ten or twelve miles an hour? This rapid voyager passes over, proceeds beyond you almost out of sight, then turns, swerving widely from right to left, repasses again in both directions, traversing repeatedly the ground, while you are travelling, or rather dragging, over the same space of about a mile only once. We are apt to exaggerate in these matters, but with every allowance, having compared the flight of a dragon-fly with that of a passing hawk, swallow, or cuckoo, I have computed that this large species is capable of flying at a speed of from eighty to one hundred miles an hour—an enormous draw upon the creature's nerves and muscular powers, as manifested by occasional rests of a few minutes upon a bush or a piece of sedge, its habits not requiring uninterrupted flight at such a pace. Perhaps the need of these occasional rests is an erroneous opinion founded upon too limited an area of observation. For Cuvier has stated that M. Poey, who had particularly studied the insects of Cuba, informed him that at certains season of the year the northerly winds bring to the city of Havannah and its neighbourhood an innumerable quantity of specimens of one of the species of *Libellulæ*. Other instances of the periodical flights or migrations of dragon-flies have been noted by observers. And even butterflies have been seen to migrate to distant points of land, making flights of fifty or sixty miles across water. These long journeys may be relieved by occasional rests, as Mr. Newman and others have ascertained that lepidopterous insects are able to alight upon the water, rest awhile, and then rise with apparent ease—a fact readily credited by fishermen, who so frequently see the green-and-grey drake and other *ephemeræ* float down stream, and, if not taken by the trout, suddenly spring up again, and resume their aerial dances. But this power of rapid movement in the dragon-fly, be the rate more or less, is in just keeping with its structure. The insect's body is slender, the chest strongly developed, though firm; the wings, four in number, are narrow, of great length, and consist of fine, thin, dry membrane, stretched upon a series of lightly made *costæ*, or rafters. No wonder, then, that with such a mechanism the creature pursues its prey of smaller insects with such rapidity.

There are many insects which one would little suspect being furnished with apparatus suited to swift and more or less continuous flight. House flies frequent the insides of our windows, buzzing sluggishly in and out of the room. But what different creatures are they when they accompany your horse on a hot summer's day. A swarm of these little pests keep pertinaciously on wing about the horse's ears; quicken the pace up to ten or twelve miles an hour, still they are there; let a gust of wind arise and carry them backwards and behind, the breeze having dropped, their speed is redoubled, and they return to their post of annoyance to the poor horse, even when urged to its fastest pace. But this example gives only a partial proof of the fly's power of flight, as the following will show. The writer was travelling one day in autumn by rail at about twenty-five miles an hour, when a company of flies put in an appearance at the carriage window. They never settled, but easily kept pace with the train; so much so, indeed, that their flight seemed to be almost mechanical, and a thought struck the writer that they had probably been drawn into a kind of vortex, whereby they were carried onward with little exertion on the part of themselves. But this notion was quickly dispelled. They sallied forth at right-angles from the carriage, flew to a distance of thirty or forty feet, still keeping pace, and then returned with increased speed and buoyancy to the window. To account for this look at the wings of a fly. Each is composed of an upper and lower membrane, between which the blood-vessels and respiratory organs ramify so as to form a delicate network for the extended wings. These are used with great quickness, and probably six hundred strokes are made per second. This would carry the fly about twenty-five feet, but a seven-fold velocity can easily be attained, making one hundred and seventy-five feet per second, so that under certain circumstances it can outstrip the fleetest racehorse. If a small insect like a fly can outstrip a racehorse, an insect as large as a horse would travel very much faster than a cannon-ball.

Bees and wasps are even swifter than flies. Here is another actual incident. The present writer has sprinkled individual wasps and bees with rose-coloured powder, and has found that thus handicapped they could with ease keep up with the fastest trains when speeding down "Shap Summit," one of the steepest gradients in the country. Nor were these carried along in the rush of air caused by the train. They would come in and out of the window, sometimes disappearing for a minute or more, but frequently returning again and again. At distances of from five to ten miles they dropped behind, when others took their places. All of us have seen the flagging, lazy butterfly, flitting from flower to flower in our gardens—not quite so lazy, however, if goaded on by some urgent motive. For when this little flutterer, touched by some strange and mysterious feeling which we cannot read, mounts on sportive wings, "through fields of air prepared to sail," she hurries onwards and onwards to some new haven of real or fancied delight and happiness. Such were the thoughts which occurred when one of these wanderers accompanied the writer by the roadside for a couple of miles, never flagging a yard behind, nay, sometimes being before a horse that was travelling at the rate of nine or ten miles an hour. What could all this speed and earnestness of the little creature mean? It is not easy to explain how the butterfly, with its broad, soft, feathery wings, should be able to accomplish the feat of speed just recorded.*

In the tropics countless swarms of locusts sometimes suddenly make their appearance, and as suddenly vanish. They cover every leaf-bearing thing, and occasionally completely denude whole districts of greenery. So great are their powers of flight that they have been seen at sea nearly four hundred miles from

* For several interesting facts concerning the flight of insects, especially the dragon-fly, I am indebted to the late Dr. Gough.

nearest land. In Natal the farmers, rightly or wrongly, believe that the locusts introduce injurious seeds upon their grass-lands, and the following would seem to show that their belief is well founded. A Mr. Weale, who was of their way of thinking, collected a packet of dried pellets and sent them to England. When closely examined under the microscope they revealed a number of tiny seeds, from which plants of seven kinds of grasses were ultimately raised.

Among animals, those which have been longest under the care of man have attained to the greatest degree of perfection in all those qualities it has been deemed wise to develop. With his mind bent on utility, man has striven to improve the staying and flying power of pigeons; the strength and swiftness of horses; and has himself proved to be a marvellous instance of speed and endurance. To observe the differences of locomotion, both as regards structural contrivance and speed among animals—the term "animal" being extended to every member, high or low, within the province of the animal kingdom—is one of the most fascinating of out-door studies. It is not an easy matter, however, to compute the speed or mileage of quick-moving animals. Among quadrupeds, the horse perhaps may be considered the fleetest. "Hambletonian" covered a space of four miles in eight minutes, which is but thirty miles an hour, if it could be continued. "Firetail" ran a mile in one minute and four seconds; and the famous "Eclipse" is said to have gone at the rate of a mile in a minute for a short distance. But it is difficult to form any exact estimate of his speed, as he never met with an opponent to put him to the test. During one of his trials, an old woman, according to Youatt, was asked if she had seen a race. Her reply was that "she could not tell whether it was a race or not, but she had seen a horse with a white leg running away at a monstrous rate, and another horse, a great way behind, trying to run after him; but she was sure he would never catch the white-legged horse, even if he ran to the world's end." The above records refer of course to horses galloping; but trotting, which is more or less an artificial mode of horse progression, has, with regard to speed, almost been reduced to an art. For facts concerning it we must look mainly to America, and perhaps no records are more interesting than those of the famous trotting mare "Maud S." On September 1st, 1884, Maud ran a mile over the Hartford track in two minutes twenty-eight seconds; and every fourth day she trotted over the same distance, the first being the slowest, and the fourth the fastest— two minutes twenty seconds. At the end of eight days her training consisted of trotting over two or three mile journeys, with the result that the time was brought down to two minutes thirteen seconds; and three days later to two minutes eleven and three-quarter seconds. Resting some days, Maud was again tried, and among other times succeeded in trotting the mile in a fraction of a second over the above, but went marvellously in the last half-mile. Subsequently to this she was shipped to Lexington, Kentucky, and when she had covered the mile distance in two minutes sixteen and a half seconds, it was decided that three days hence she should endeavour to beat her own great record. This she succeeded in doing by trotting a mile in two minutes nine and a half seconds; and a year later Maud made the world's record—two minutes eight and three-quarter seconds. This is what no other horse ever accomplished, and the interesting phase of the situation is that the mare is even now in training to beat her own splendid record given above.

As compared to the rate of speed in animals, those attained by man are interesting. A hundred yards has been run in ten seconds; two hundred yards in twenty and two-fifths; three hundred yards in thirty-one and a half; and a quarter of a mile in forty-eight and four-fifths seconds, by Messrs. A. Wharton, J. Shearman, C. G. Wood, and L. E. Myers respectively. Mr. W. G. George holds the championship for one mile and up to ten miles; his time for the former distance being four minutes eighteen and two-fifths seconds, and for the latter fifty-one minutes twenty seconds.

For fifteen, twenty, and twenty-five miles Mr. G. A. Dunning holds the record; the first distance being covered in one hour twenty-four minutes and twenty-four seconds; the last in two hours thirty-three minutes forty seconds. The same gentleman is champion at forty miles. Mr. J. A. Squires has run thirty miles in three hours seventeen minutes thirty-six and a-half seconds; and Mr. J. E. Dixon is fifty-mile champion with six hours eighteen minutes and twenty-six and one-fifth seconds — all truly marvellous performances.

CHAPTER V.

THE SNOW-WALKERS.

THIS morning—
> We looked upon a world unknown,
> On nothing we could call our own.
> Around the glistening wonder bent
> The blue walls of the firmament;
> No cloud above, no earth below,
> A universe of sky and snow.

The sun shines, and a rosy suffusion is over the landscape. All the fences are buried deep, and the trees stand starkly outlined against the sky. Millions of snow-crystals glint athwart the fields. Birds swarm in the garden—the home birds more confiding and the wild birds tame. Tits hang to the suet bags, and a general assembly flock to the cornsheaf. A ring-ouzel flies wildly from the rowan-tree, and four or five species of thrushes are among the berries of the shrubs.

So softly winnowed is the falling snow that it scarce bends the few grasses and dead plants that now appear above its surface. The kindly snow obliterates the torn and abraded scars of

The Snow-Walkers.

nature; but it not the less effectually reproduces the prints of her children. To the light the snow reveals the doings of the night. Does a mouse so much as cross, she leaves her delicate tracery on the white coverlet. Away from the homestead rabbits have crossed and recrossed the fields in a perfect maze. That ill-defined "pad" tracks a hare to the turnips. Pheasants and wood-pigeons have scratched for mast beneath the beeches, and we find red blood-drops along the fence. These are tracked to a colony of weasels in the old wall. Last night a piteous squeal might have been heard from the half-buried fence, and the little tragedy would be played out upon the snow. Five wild swans cleave the thin air far up, and fly off with outstretched necks. The tiny brown wren bids defiance to the weather; darting in and out of every hole and crevice, usually reappearing with the cocoon of some insect in its bill. These delicate footprints reproduce the long toes of the lark, and those are the tracks of the meadow pipit. The hedge-berries are almost gone; and here the redwing and fieldfare have run along the fence bottom in search of fallen fruit. Those larger tracks by the sheep troughs show that the hungry rooks have been scratching near, and the chatter of magpies comes from the fir-tree tops. Scattered pine cones betoken a flock of incessantly chattering crossbills; and once in the fir wood we caught a glimpse of the scarlet appendages of the rare Bohemian waxwing. The gaudily-coloured yellow-hammer shows well against the snow, and bathes its orange plumage in the feathered rain. How our British finches seem to enjoy the frost and snow! Certain it is that now their stores of food become scant; but then they throw in their lot with the sparrows of barn-door and rick-yard. The bright bachelor finch stands out from his pure setting, and the daws look black against the snow. " Tweet," " tweet," comes through the cold thin air, and is startling in its stillness ; and now we may hear as well as see the flight of a flock of linnets and goldfinches. Here observe a tall, nodding thistle-head, its once dark green leaves shrivelled up and turned to grey, its purple flower-rays to russet brown. They contain ripened seeds. A goldfinch hangs to the under surface, and a rose-breasted linnet clings to the topmost spray. The two frail things are not unlike in form, though the goldfinch is by far the handsomer bird. His prettily-shaped beak is flesh-coloured, as are also his legs. His head has patches of scarlet, white, and black, each well defined and setting off the other. The breast and back are of varying tints of warm russet brown, and the feathers of the wing are picked out with orange. His tail is alternately elevated and depressed as he changes his position ; and the patches of golden yellow are well brought out as he flutters from spray to spray. Thus do the linnet and the goldfinch go through the winter, together ranging the fields, and feeding upon the seeds they can pick up.

Along the meadow brook a stately heron has left its imprints; the water-hen's track is marked through the reeds; and there upon the icy margin are the blurred webs of wild ducks. A bright red squirrel runs along the white wall. In its warm furs it shows sharply against the fence. Naturalists say that the squirrel hibernates through the winter; but this is hardly so. A bright day, even though cold and frosty, brings him out to visit some summer store. The prints of the squirrel are sharply cut, the tail at times just brushing the snow. The mountain linnets have come down to the lowlands; and we flush a flock from an ill-farmed field where weeds run rampant. When alarmed the birds wheel aloft, uttering the while soft twitterings, then betake themselves to the trees. The seeds of brooklime, flax, and knapweed the twite seems partial to, and this wild-weed field is to them a very paradise. Just now, walking in the woods, the cry of the bullfinch is heard as perhaps the most melancholy of all our birds, but its bright scarlet breast compensates for its want of cheeriness. A flock of diminutive gold-crests rush past us, and in the fir wood we hear but cannot see a flock of siskins.

Higher up the valley, towards the hills, tracks of another kind begin to appear. On the fells we come across a dead herdwick, trampled about with innumerable feet. We examine these closely, and find that they are only of two species—the raven and the buzzard. Further in the scrub we track a pine-marten to its lair in the rocks. The dogs drive it from its stronghold, and, being arboreal in its habits, it immediately makes up the nearest pine trunk. Its rich brown fur and orange throat make it one of the most lithely beautiful of British animals. A pair of stoats or ermines, with their flecked coats just in the transition stage, have their haunt in the same wood. From the snow we see that last night they have threaded the aisles of the pines in search of food. This clear-cut sharp track by the fence is that of a fox.

Another fascinating aspect of nature in winter are the woods. When snow-covered there is a grandeur and majesty about them such as they never wear at other times. The giant limbs of the trees stand starkly outlined against the sky, and nought but sound silence possesses the aisles of plumed pines. Except the faint trickle of the stream, it would seem almost as though the pulse of nature had ceased to beat. Of course, this only applies to the interior of the woods, and the suggestion is emphasised by the thick soft carpetings of pine needles

The Snow-Walkers. 91

where these have dropped for many tree-generations.

Once again we are enjoying the pleasure of wild shooting in winter, but now in the open glades. Again there has been a slight fall of snow, and, sure, morning was never more beautiful. The feathered rain is crisp to the tread, and the warm sun converts the air to that of summer. The sea is blue, the hills rose-tinted, and the snow-crystals make the landscape gloriously, dazzlingly bright. A coating of snow will always arrest the eye of the observant sportsman, more especially if he have a *penchant* for natural history. There are the tracks and trails of birds and animals, and what zest is added to the search in the possibility of finding a new one! Only those who follow the tracks of the snow-walkers know really how rich is the land in all animate nature. Be the stitching on the white coverlet never so faint or so delicate, it is always rendered faithfully. In the snow we read out the history of the wild creatures immediately about us, the existence of which we never even suspected. In our home fields there are two or three mice, as many shrews, and a couple of voles. These latter leave their tracks in the hedge bottoms, or along the stream sides, and we see not only where they have burrowed, but what they have eaten. The shrews and mice are on dryer ground, and their delicate feet have pencilled the prettiest patterns upon the snow. The tracks of the partridge are pretty, too, and from them we read what ceaseless runners the birds are. A depression shows where they have roosted last night, and then their tracks may be followed through the stubble and seed fields. By the brook-side are the hair-like tracings of innumerable small birds; and the water margins here record the fullest registering. This may be owing to the soft brook banks and their aquatic life, when the rest of the fields are icebound. Then many of the spawning fish are still on the redds, and the prospect of these may be an additional inducement to some of the fish-feeding creatures. Here, clutching a tuft of couch-grass is a dead barn-owl, for which the intense cold has proved too much—one enemy less to the shrews and field mice, whose hasty tracks here and there show that more than once last night they have had to beat a hasty retreat. Once during the day, as the ferrets were turned into a burrow, some one pointed out a brace of ermines that had doubtless been looking after the rabbits on their own account. They were still in their brown summer fur, and made their way over the snow and out of harm's way at a remarkably rapid rate. This little incident reminds us of a brown owl which emerged from a rabbit-hole just as the ermines did, and curiously enough these birds had a couple of eggs and a young one even in December, with the ground snow-covered. The heavy blurred tracks of grouse were at first difficult to determine, and the key to them was only to be found in the birds themselves, as they rose with a startling whirr. They had been driven from the higher to the lower ground in search of food. One of the terriers disintered a spiny hedgehog from its warm, leafy retreat, and "Prickles" probably felt much mystified to find himself in a world of dazzling whiteness.

There was one other track which it would be long and devious to follow—one which had been abroad under the moon and stars, and from its trail would seem to have known the ways and the haunts of both furred and feathered game by heart—and that was the old poacher. The snow is a great tell-tale, but it causes the poacher's eye to grow keen and his step firm; and nothing but the gaol walls will prevent his being a snow-walker. His life has been one long protest against the game laws; and whatever he is, or is not, he believes them to be unjust.

CHAPTER VI.

WHEN DARKNESS HAS FALLEN.

A TIME of absolute quiet can never be observed in the country. It matters not as to time and season; there seems to be no general period of repose. There is always something abroad, some creature of the fields and woods, which by its voice or movements is betrayed. Just as in an old rambling house there are always strange noises that cannot be accounted for, so in the by-paths of nature there are innumerable sounds which can never be localised. To those, however, who pursue night avocations in the country—gamekeepers, poachers, and others—there are always calls and cries which bespeak life as animate under the night as that of the day. This is attributable to various animals and birds, to night-flying insects, and even to fish. Let us track some of these sounds to their source.

"When comes still evening on, and twilight

grey hath in her sober liv'ry all things clad," then it is that the white owl comes abroad. Passing the remains of an old baronial hall, its piercing screech comes from the dismantled tower. Here the owls have lived time out of mind, and we have seen and heard them, asleep and awake, through every hour of the day and night. It is unnatural history to assert, as Mr. Gray does, that the barn-owls ever mope or mourn or are melancholy. Neither are they grave monks nor anchorites nor pillared saints. A boding bird or a dolorous! Nonsense, they are none of these. They issue forth as very devils, and like another spirit of the night, sail about seeking whom they may devour. The barn-owl is the "screech" owl of bird literature; the brown owl the true hooting owl. This species is found in heavily-timbered districts, and it particularly loves the dark and sombre gloom of resinous pine woods. But the barn-owl is only the precursor of new life—life as animate under the night, as that of the birds and butterflies under the day. We follow the path by the river, and on through the meadows. Among the nut-bush tops a bat is hawking for night-flying insects. Great white moths get up from the grass and go looming away through the darkness. A bend in the stream brings us to a quiet river reach with brown pebbles and a shallow.

A sentinel heron that has been standing watchful on one leg rises, and flaps languidly away down the river reach. The consumptive figure of the gaunt bird stands by the stream through all weathers. He knows not times nor seasons, and is a great poacher. In the wind, when taking his lone stand, his loose fluttering feathers look like drift-stuff caught in the bushes. He reminds one of the consumptive, but, unlike him, has wonderful powers of digestion, and withal an immense capacity for fish. Woe to the luckless mort or trout that comes within reach of his formidable pike, or to the attacking peregrine that he attempts to impale on his bill. The heron is essentially a wanderer, and, like Wordsworth's immortal leech-gatherer, he roams from pond to pond, from moor to moor. Herons come and go by the same routes; and night after night have we flushed our fisher from the selfsame shallow.

The peculiarly wild whistle of the curlew comes from out the night sky, and swifts screech for an hour after darkness has fallen. We are now by the covert side, and a strange churring sound comes from out the darkened glades. Waiting silently beneath the bushes, it approaches nearer and nearer until a loud flapping is heard in the bushes. The object approaches quite closely, and it is seen that the noise is produced by a large bird striking its wings together as they meet behind. Even in the darkness it may be detected that each wing is crossed by a definite white bar. The bird is a goatsucker or nightjar. Had we it in our hand, we should see that it was a connecting link between the owls and the swallows, having the soft plumage and noiseless flight of the one and the wide gape of the other. The object of the noise it produces is probably to disturb from the bushes the large nightflying moths upon which it feeds. The name goatsucker the bird has from a superstitious notion that it sucks goats and cows —a myth founded probably upon the fact of its wide gape. It is certain that these birds may often be seen flitting about the bellies of cattle as they stand knee-deep in the summer pastures. The reason of this is obvious, as there insect food is always abundant. Unless disturbed, the nightjar rarely comes abroad during the day, but obtains its food at twilight and dusk. Upon the limestone-covered fells it conforms marvellously to its environment, it being almost impossible to detect its curiously mottled plumage as it basks upon the grey stones, not more still than itself. Here it lays its two eggs, often without the slightest semblance of a nest, frequently upon the bare rock. Quite a peculiar interest attaches to the bird, inasmuch as it is furnished with a remarkable claw, the use of which is guessed at rather than known. This claw is serrated on its inner edge, and from actual experiments made upon nightjars in captivity, we should surmise that its use is to free the long whiskers from the soft, silvery dust which usually covers the bodies of night-flying moths. Certain it is that this substance gets upon the whiskers of the bird, and that the long hairs referred to are combed through the serrated claw. About the mouth the goat-sucker is very swallow-like. It has a bullet-shaped head, large eyes, and a wide gape. Like the swallows, too, it has a weak, ineffective bill, and weak feet. This is explained by the fact that the bird, except when nesting, is rarely seen on the ground, and that it captures its insect prey on the wing. From twilight till grey does the fern-owl "churr" and fly through the night.

As we proceed, a splash comes from the river, and some large-winged fly has been sucked under. The night food comes on, and the reach boils. Water-rats, voles, and shrews are busy among the stones searching for insect larvæ, or gnawing the stalks of water-plants. The wafting of wings overhead betokens a curlew flying through the darkness to its feeding ground. The peculiarly lonely wail of the summer-snipe comes down stream, and a teal stretches her neck low over the sand. The river here resolves itself into a gorge, and runs deep betwixt shelving rocks. The water ceaselessly moans and chafes down there in the darkness. Badgers have their haunt deep in the brambles, their tortuous burrows running far out among the boulders. From the tree-tops we may watch them digging for roots and wasps' nests, and now and then snapping at flies. Passing the deep dub by the "Force," we find old Phil, the fisher, plying his silent trade even thus into the night. Phil leads his own life, and is contemplative as becomes his craft. Nature's every sight and sound he has, as it were, by heart, and he makes friends even with the creeping things. As we watch, a salmon, fresh from the sea, leaps from the silvery foam and flashes in the moonlight.

One of the greatest night-helps to the gamekeeper in staying the depredations of poachers is the lapwing. It is the lightest sleeper of the fields, starting up from the fallows and screaming upon the slightest alarm. Poachers dread the detection of this bird, and the keeper closely follows its cry. A hare rushing wildly past will put the plover away from its roost; and when hares act thus in the darkness, there is generally some good cause for it. The skylark and and woodlark are both occasional night-singers, and it is common to hear cuckoos call in the densest darkness. Still we follow on. Rabbits have made pitfalls in the loose, yellow sand, and we see their white scuts as vanishing points in the darkness. Mice rustle away, and a hedgehog comes to the pool to drink. One of the latter we saw just now taken in the keeper's trap, the latter baited with a pheasant's egg. The squeal of a foumart comes from the loose stones. Later it will feed on the frogs now croaking from the ditch; these it kills by piercing their skulls.

If the cuckoo tells her name to all the hills, so does the sedge-warbler to the fluted reeds. And, like that wandering voice, our little bird seems dispossessed of a corporeal existence, and on through summer is "still longed for, never seen" —and this though common enough, for you may wander long among the willows, with a bird in every bush, without one showing outside its corral of boughs. Wherever vegetation grows tall and luxuriant, there the "reed-wren" may be found. It travels in the night: you go out some May morning, and the rollicking intoxication of the garrulous little bird comes from out the self-same bush from which you missed it in autumn. From the time it first arrives it begins to sing louder and louder as the warm weather advances, especially in the evenings. Then it is that it listens to the loud-swelling bird-choir of the woods, selecting a note from this and another from that; for the sedge-warbler is an imitator, a mocking bird, and reproduces in fragments the songs of many species. The little mimic runs up and down the gamut in the most riotous fashion, parodying not only the loud, clear whistle of the blackbird, but the wholly differing soft, sweet notes of the willow-wren. This is kept up through the night, and the puzzle is when the little musician sleeps. If the sedge-warbler ceases its song through any hour of the day or night, a clod thrown into the bushes will immediately set it going again. Yet what can be said of a song that a clod of earth will produce? Sometimes for a moment it is sweet, but never long-sustained. In the North, where there are few ditches, the species frequents river-banks and the sides of tarns; in the South, it abounds everywhere in marshy places. Here the rank grass swarms with them; the thicker the reed-patch or willow, the more birds are there. With perfect silence, a distant view of the bird is sometimes obtained at the top of the bushes, as it flits after an insect. As it runs up and clings to the tall grass stalks, it is pleasing both in form and colour. Among the grasses and water-plants it has its game preserves. Water-beetles, ephemeræ, and the teeming aquatic insects constitute its food. To watch through a glass the obtaining of these is most interesting. Reed-sparrow and reed-wren are pretty provincial names of the bird, each expressive enough.

A powerful perfume rises from the ground-weeds, and stooping low, we detect dame's violet. The purple *Hesperis matronalis* emits its sweet smell only at night, and is fertilised by moths. This, too, holds good of the evening campion (*Lychins vespertina*), only its scent is fainter. For this, however, the colour of its white petals amply compensates, as they are more easily seen in the darkness. Further on, we detect *Orchis bifolia*, which is also particularly sweet, and with the same object. All these emit fragrance at night, and are fertilised *only* by night-flying insects. A crash! the underwood is rudely torn, and a form disappears in the darkness. The crackling of boughs and dead sticks mark on the stillness of night the poacher's sinuous path through the woods. Soon his old black bitch slinks by the hedge, clears the fence at a bound, and doggedly follows her master's footsteps. Crake answers crake from the meadows as they have done through the night. Now they are at our feet, now far out yonder. The night call of the partridge comes from the gorse, and the first pheasant crows from the larch branches. On the hill we wade through a herd of recumbent heifers, their sketchy forms sharply outlined in the darkness. These are quietly chewing the cud, and turn upon us their great soft eyes; some even press their dewy noses against us. The sweet breath of kine is wafted on the night, and the drone of many insects.

It is wonderful how lightly the creatures of the fields and woods sleep. The faintest rustle brings chirping from the bushes, and in the densest darkness the wood pigeons coo. Jays screech in the glade, and the wood-owls hoot. One of the essentially night-singers is the grasshopper warbler. Shy and retiring in its habits, it is rarely found far distant from aquatic vegetation. Moist situations are most congenial, as among the plants that effect them it finds its winged food. Although generally effecting such spots as indicated, it sometimes seeks out considerable elevations. These are covered with coarse grass, bent, furze, and heather; and here, far into the night, it reels out its continuous cricket-like song. It returns to the same spot year after year, and although from these the particular notes may be often heard, the singer itself is nowhere to be seen. At the least noise it drops from the support on which it may be depending into the grass beneath, then is silent. The song is long continued, but the sounds are constantly shifting, marking the restless track of the singer on the night. It needs no stretch of imagination to detect in the notes of this species the similarity to the grasshopper, and the "monotonous whirr like the spinning of a fishing-reel," is fairly expressible of the bird's song. Perfect master of intricate maze and covert, it is never far from them. Even though it has ventured above his accustomed limits, its vigilance sends it back at the least noise, though its retreat is rarely observed, for instead of flying, it creeps closely, never rising when alarmed. Again we pass into the darkness. Moles have thrown up ridges of loose, light soil; and these cross us again and again. The short, sharp bark of a fox comes from the scrub; and soon dog and vixen answer each other across the dale.

And now we enter the park. The deer, disturbed in the darkness, get up and walk quietly away. A white fawn is outlined against the dark herd. Whenever an owner dies, say the menials at the Hall, a great bough is riven from the giant oak; whenever a new heir comes to the estate, a white fawn is born. Under the dark slabs by the river the otters breed; but it is impossible to dislodge them. Iron-sinewed, shaggy otter-hounds have tried, but never with success. The fishermen complain of the quantity of fish which the otter destroys. Trout are found dead on the rocks; salmon are there bitten in the shoulder, but only partially eaten. The evolutions of the otter in its native element are the poetry of motion minus only the metre.

When almost the whole of the insect-world has folded its wings in sleep, there is a class of night-flyers whose hours of activity are those of darkness. Among the more interesting of these is the male glow-worm—the English lantern-fly —whose light may be plainly seen as he flits past, pale and ghostly against the dark background of some deeply-foliaged bank or shadowy wood. Then there is the great army of night-flying moths, whose nocturnal wanderings present such a weird appearance in the darkness, and whose life-history contrasts so sharply with the sunny dalliance of their butterfly cousins. As moths have to contend with the night winds their constitution is more robust than that of the *rhopolocera*, or day-fliers. Their bodies are thicker, their wings narrower and more strongly nerved. As they settle themselves on corrugated bark or grey stones to their deep, diurnal sleep, their sober and inconspicuous colouring invariably saves them even from detection. In many species this daily trance is so profound that a slumbering insect may be transfixed and never detect the occurrence until twilight again comes round. But if the closely-folded upper wings are quiet and sober in colouring this is only for protective reasons; for brilliant toilets are presented when twilight falls and affords its dewy veil. Under the closely-folded wings of dusky grey are bright bodices of red, scarlet, crimson, and orange. What an admirable chapter "The Loves of the Night-Flyers" would afford by one who had fondly watched the fairy things through the dewy hours of a short summer night.

The twilight-flyers afford a distinct class to the night-flyers, and have several well-marked characteristics. These are termed hawk-moths, and have long, sharp, scythe-like wings. The death's-head moth, the largest and most interesting British species, belongs to this group. It seldom comes abroad before darkness has fallen, and is always conspicuous in its nocturnal flight. Linnæus, following his habitual system of nomenclature, placed this insect in the "sphinx" family on account of the form of its magnificent caterpillar, and gave it the specific name of *Atropos*, in allusion to the popular superstition. Atropos being, according to Hesiod, the one of the fates whose office it was to cut the thread of human life, spun by her sisters, Clotho and Lachesis. Modern entomologists have preserved the idea of Linnæus, giving to the new genus the name of *acherontia*—pertaining to Acheron, one of the streams which, in the Greek mythology, have to be passed before entering the infernal regions. A low, wailing sound which this insect emits has greatly added to the terror which its appearance inspires among ignorant rustics. The death's-head moth is a really splendid insect. Its stretched wings cover four and a half inches, and it is the largest of the British Lepidoptera. As is well known, it has its popular name from a marvellously good representation of a skull and crossbones upon the upper part of the thorax—a mark which has caused it to be an object of dread in every country which it inhabits. Fluttering at the window in the darkness, or entering the house by the open door, just after the close of twilight, it is considered a certain omen of death. Like the hoarse croak of the raven, and the "boding" hoot of the owl, the appearance of this moth is said to be followed by disease and death. The power possessed by the death's-head insect of emitting a shrill, creaking sound, is thought to be unique among the British Lepidoptera, and each time the strange sound is emitted, the whole body gives a convulsive sort of start. The insect can be induced to utter this strange note by being irritated.

Another especially interesting night-flyer is the ghost moth. Just as the twilight of a summer evening is deepening into darkness, and a soft, warm wind stirs the foliage of the woods, the ghost moth comes abroad. The observer sees a fitful apparition which suddenly vanishes into space. First a large insect with long wings is seen advancing, it comes straight on, then flutters in the air—and is gone. Whilst endeavouring to discover the mysterious retreat of the moth, it will suddenly reappear, and even whilst the eye closely follows its flight, will again vanish. This effect is produced by the different colour of the wings on their upper and lower sides. Above they are snowy white, and consequently visible even in the deep twilight; but on the under side they, as well as the whole body, are of a deep dusky brown so that when that side is suddenly turned towards the spectator it becomes invisible. As the male flies in the night, the white shining upper surface of the wings glitters curiously, almost appearing as if they were giving out their own light.

Standing in one of the rides of a woodland glade just as day is departing, one is pierced, thrilled by a perfect storm of song. This loud swelling volume of sound softens as the darkness deepens, and then only the polyglot wood-thrush is heard. The stem of the silver birch has ceased to vibrate to the blackbird's whistle, and as darkness comes a new set of sounds take possession of the night. But passing down through the meadows we have other thoughts than listening to these.

Another night singer is the blackcap. The

flute-like mellowness and wild sweetness of its song give it a high place among British warblers—next only to the nightingale. The blackcap has neither the fulness nor the force, but it has all and more of the former's purity. This little hideling, with its timid obtrusiveness, never strays far from cultivation. One provision it requires, and this is seclusion. Its shy and retiring habits teach it to search out dense retreats, and it is rarely seen. If observed on the confines of its corral of boughs it immediately begins to perform a series of evolutions until it has placed a dense screen of brushwood between itself and the observer.

Many times have we heard the round, full, lute-like plaintiveness of the nightingale, sounds that seem to seize and ingrain themselves in the very soul, that "make the wild blood start in its mystic springs." To us the delicious triumph of the bird's song lies in its utter *abandon*. The lute-like sweetness, the silvery liquidness, the bubbling and running over, and the wild, gurgling "jug, jug, jug!" To say this, and more—that the nightingale is a mad, sweet polyglot, that it is the sweetest of English warblers, the essence and quintessence of song, that it is the whole wild bird achievement in one—these are feeble, feeble! This "light-winged dryad of the trees" is still "in some melodious spot of beechen green and shadows numberless, singing of summer in full-throated ease," and here she will remain. Unlike the songs of some of our warblers, hers can never be reproduced. Attempt to translate it, and it eludes you, only its meagre skeleton remains. Isaac Walton, in his quaint eloquence, tries to say what he felt: "The nightingale, another of my airy creatures, breathes such sweet, loud music out of her little instrumental throat, that it might make mankind to think miracles are not ceased. He that at midnight . . . . should hear, as I have very often, the clear airs, the sweet descants, the natural rising and falling, the doubling and redoubling of her voice, might well be lifted above earth, and say, 'Lord, what music hast Thou provided for the saints in heaven, when Thou affordest bad men such music on earth!'"

Although Britain can show no parallel either in number or brilliance to the living lights of the tropics, we are not without several interesting phosphorescent creatures of our own. Those whose business leads them abroad in the fields and woods through the short summer nights are often treated to quite remarkable luminous sights. Last night the writer was lying on a towering limestone escarpment, waiting to intercept a gang of poachers. The darkness was dead and unrelieved, and a warm rain studded every grass blade with moisture. When the day and sun broke, this would glow with a million brilliant prismatic colours, then suddenly vanish. But the illumination came sooner, and in a different way. The rain ceased, and hundreds of tiny living lights lit up the sward. In the intense darkness these shone with an unusual brilliancy, and lit up the almost impalpable moisture. Every foot of ground was studded with its star-like gem, and these twinkled and shone as the fireflies stirred in the grass. The sight was quite an un-English one, and the soft green glow only paled at the coming of day. One phase of this interesting phenomenon is that now we can have a reproduction of it nightly. The fireflies were collected, turned down on the lawn, and their hundred luminous lamps now shed a soft lustre over all the green.

Why our British fireflies are designated "glow-worms" is difficult to understand. *Lampyris noctiluca* has nothing worm-like about it. It is a true insect. The popular misconception has probably arisen in this wise. The female glow-worm, the light-giver, is wingless; the male is winged. The latter, however, has but little of the light emitting power possessed by the female. Only the light-givers are collected, and being destitute of the first attribute of an insect, wings, are set down in popular parlance as worms. Old mossy banks, damp hedgerows, and shaded woods are the loved haunts of the fireflies, and the warm nights of the soft summer months most induce them to burn their soft lustre. Some widowed worm or firefly flirt may shed her luminous self in the darkness even on into dying summer or autumn. But this is unusual. It is not definitely known what purpose is served by the emission of the soft green light, but it has long been suspected that the lustre was to attract the male. Gilbert White found that glow-worms were attracted by the light of candles, and many of them came into his parlour. Another naturalist by the same process captured as many as forty male glow-worms in an evening. Still another suggestion is that the phosphorescence serves for a protection or means of defence to the creatures possessing it, and an incident which seems to support this view has been actually witnessed. This was in the case of a carabeus which was observed running round and round a phosphorescent centipede, evidently wishing but not daring to attack it. A third explanation of the phenomenon is that it serves to afford light for the creature to see by. A somewhat curious confirmation of this is the fact that in the insect genus to which our British fireflies belong, the *Lampyridæ*, the degree of luminosity is exactly in inverse proportion to the development of the vision.

When Darkness has fallen.

Fireflies glow with greatest brilliancy at midnight. Their luminosity is first seen soon after dark:

> "The glow-worm shows the matin to be near,
> And 'gins to pale his ineffectual fire."

As the insects rest on the grass and moss, the difference in the amount of light emitted is quite marked. While the luminous spot indicated by a female is quite bright, the males show only as the palest fire. When on the wing, the light of the latter is not seen at all. Heavy rain, so long as it is warm, serves only to increase the brightness. The seat of the light of the glow-worm is in the tail, and proceeds from three luminous sacs in the last segment of the abdomen. The male has only two of these, and the light proceeding from them is comparatively small. During favourable weather the light glows steadily, but at other times it is not constant. The fireflies of the tropics—those comprising the genus *Lampyridæ*—vary to the extent that while certain species control their light, others are without this power. The light of our English glow-worm is undoubtedly under its control, as upon handling the insect it is immediately put out. It would seem to take some little muscular effort to produce the luminosity, as one was observed to move continually the last segment of the body so long as it continued to shine. The larvæ of the glow-worm is capable of emitting light, but not to be compared to that of the developed insect. Both in its nature and immature forms, *Lampyris noctiluca* plays a useful part in the economy of Nature. To the agriculturist and fruit-grower it is a special friend. Its diet consists almost wholly of small shelled snails, and it comes upon the scene just as these farm and garden pests are most troublesome. British fireflies probably have never yet figured as personal ornaments to female beauty. This is, and has always been, one of their uses to the dusky daughters of the tropics. They are often studded in the coiled and braided hair, and perform somewhat the same office as diamonds for more civilised belles. Spanish ladies and those of the West Indies enclose fireflies in bags of lace or gauze, and wear them amid their hair or disposed about their persons. The luminosity of our modest English insect is far outshone by several of its congeners. Some of these are used in various ways for illumination, and it is said that the brilliancy of the light is such that the smallest print can be read by that proceeding from the thoracic spots alone, when a single insect is moved along the lines. In the Spanish settlements, the fireflies are frequently used in a curious way when travelling at night. The natives tie an insect to each great toe; and on fishing and hunting expeditions make torches of them by fastening several together. The same people have a summer festival at which the garments of the young people are covered with fireflies, and being mounted on fine horses similarly ornamented, the latter gallop through the dusk, the whole producing the effect of a large moving light.

Another phosphorescent little creature found commonly in Britian is a centipede with the expressive name *Geophilus electricus*. This is a tiny living light which shows its luminous qualities in a remarkable and interesting fashion. It may not uncommonly be seen on field and garden paths, and leaves a lovely train of phosphorescent fire as it goes. This silvery train glows in the track of the insect, sometimes extending to twenty inches in length. In addition to this, its phosphorescence is exhibited by a row of luminous spots on each side its body, and these points of pale fire present quite a pretty sight when seen under favourable circumstances. It has been stated that the light-giving quality of the fireflies might be designed to serve them to see by; but this fails to apply to the little creature under notice, as it is without eyes.

There are still other British insects which have the repute of being phosphorescent, although the evidence is not yet quite satisfactory. Among them are the male cricket and "daddy-long-legs," both of which are reported to have been seen in a phosphorescent condition. But if there is a dearth of phosphorescent land creatures which are native, this has no application to the numerous luminous creatures living in our Southern British seas. Among marine animals the phenomenon is more general and much more splendid than anything which can be seen on land, as witness the following picture by Professor Martin Duncan: "Great domes of pale gold, with long streamers, move slowly along in endless procession; small silvery discs swim, now enlarging and now contracting; and here and there a green or bluish gleam marks the course of a tiny but rapidly rising and sinking globe. Hour after hour the procession passes by, and the fishermen hauling in their nets, from the midst drag out liquid light, and the soft sea jellies, crushed and torn piecemeal, shine in every clinging particle. The night grows dark, the wind rises and is cold, and the tide changes, so does the luminosity of the sea. The pale spectres sink deeper and are lost to sight, but the increasing waves are tinged here and there with green and white, and often along a line, where the fresh water is mixing with the salt in an estuary, there is brightness so intense that boats and shores are visible. But if such sights are to be seen on the surface, what must not be the phosphorescence of the depths ! Every sea-pen is glorious in its light ; in fact, nearly every eight-armed alcyonarian is thus resplendent, and the social pyrosoma, bulky and a free swimmer, glows like a bar of hot metal with a white and green radiance."

CHAPTER VII.

BRITISH BIRDS, THEIR NESTS AND EGGS.

OOLOGY may be said to be the latest of the sciences; and although perhaps not a very profound one, it is certainly among the most interesting. Those who are not ornithologists, or specially interested in natural history, can have but little idea of the progress made of late in all that pertains to the nidification of British birds. Expensive and elaborately illustrated treatises have been written on the subject; naturalists have spent thousands of pounds in tracking birds to their breeding haunts; and some of the best scientific workers of the day are devoting their lives to this and the kindred subject of migration. Then again city "naturalists" have their continental collectors, and are building up quite a commerce about the subject. The money value of a complete set of clutches of eggs of British birds is about £200, although more than double this sum would be given for eggs taken within the British Islands. Of course a great number of birds do not breed and never have bred here; for whilst the number of species comprising the home list is three hundred and sixty-seven, only about two hundred breed within our shores.

Not a few of the eggs of British birds are worth more than their weight in gold, whilst those of certain species which are supposed to have become extinct bring quite fabulous prices. A well-marked pair of golden eagle's eggs have been known to fetch £25. The market value of an egg of the swallow-tailed kite is three guineas, of Pallas's sand-grouse thirty shillings, while ten times that amount was recently offered for an egg of this Asiatic species taken in Britain. On the other hand, the eggs of certain of the social breeding birds are so common in their season as to be systematically collected for domestic purposes. And this in face of the fact that many of them are remarkable alike for size, shape, and beauty of colouring. This applies particularly to the guillemot, whose eggs are often remarkably handsome. As a rule the colour of these is bluish green, heavily blotched, and streaked with brown or black; and the form that of an elongated handsome pear. The guillemot is one of our commonest cliff-birds, and is found in greatest abundance at Flamborough Head. The eggs are systematically gathered by men who are let down the rocks in ropes. They traverse the narrowest ledges, placing the eggs which they gather daily in baskets fastened round their shoulders. The guillemot makes no nest, lays but one egg, and incubation lasts about a month. The birds sit upright, and when suddenly alarmed, as by the firing of a gun, the eggs fall in showers into the sea. Most of those collected at Flamborough are sent to Leeds, where the albumen is used in the preparation of patent leather; whilst the eggs taken on Lundy are used at Bristol in the manufacture of sugar. At the British breeding-stations of the gannet, or Solan goose, thousands of birds breed annually, though in numbers less than formerly. In this case the young birds, not the eggs, are taken; and on North Barra from two thousand to three thousand birds are captured in a season. The collector kills the gannets as they are taken from the nests, and they are then thrown into the sea beneath, where a boat is in waiting to pick them up. In the Faroes the people keep January 25 as a festival in consequence of the return of the birds.

The difference in size and colour which the eggs of different birds exhibit is even more apparent than the great diversity of shape. The giant eggs of wild swans and geese, or the extinct great auk, are tremendous when compared with those of the warblers and titmice; while the egg of the golden-crested wren is smaller still. This, the smallest British bird, is a mere fluff of feathers, and weighs only eighty grains. The relative sizes of the eggs named are as a garden-pea to a cocoanut. Another interesting phase of the subject is the number of eggs laid by different species. The Solan goose, guillemot, cormorant, shag, puffin, and others lay but one egg; whilst some of the tiny tits have been known to produce as many as twenty. In this respect the game-birds and wild-fowl are also prolific, and a partridge's nest containing from fifteen to twenty eggs is not at all an uncommon occurrence. Where a greater number of eggs than this is found, it is probable that two females have laid in the same nest. Certain species, again, habitually bred once, twice, or thrice a season; whilst others less prolific have but a single egg, and lay but once during the year.

Almost as interesting as the eggs they contain are the nests themselves. Birds of the plover kind almost invariably deposit their eggs in a mere depression in the ground; while many of the shore-haunting birds lay theirs in sand and shingle — often upon the bare stones. The present writer once found a ringed dotterell's nest on a bank of *débris*, the eggs being stuck right on end, and absolutely resembling the drift stuff. The lapwing's eggs invariably have their smaller ends pointing inward. This bird is an early breeder, and eggs may often be found by the middle of March. It is these first clutches that fetch such fancy prices in the market, as much as fifteen shillings having been paid for a single egg. So anxious are the poulterers to obtain these that one of them expressed himself to the effect that if he were assured of having the first ten eggs he would not hesitate to give five pounds for them. Among birds the ground builders are the most primitive architects; but their very obtrusiveness certainly aids them to escape detection. Partridges and pheasants almost invariably lay their olive eggs upon dead oak-leaves, and, moreover, cover them when they leave the nest. The red speckled eggs of the grouse are very much of the colour of the heather, as are those of wild ducks to the green reeds and rushes. The nest of the cushat, or woodpigeon, consists of a mere platform of sticks, and the eggs may almost always be seen through the interstices of the crossed twigs. The goatsucker makes no nest, but lays its eggs among burning bits of limestone on the sides of the fells; and that of the golden plover is equally non-existent. Among tree builders the jay is slovenly and negligent, while the scarlet bullfinch is equally careless. Hawks, falcons, and birds of the crow kind construct substantial platforms of sticks; though the crafty magpie is an exception, and constructs a domed nest. The reason for this is not easy to understand, but, being an arrant thief itself, the pie is perhaps suspicious of birddom in general. The pretty water-ouzel, or dipper, also builds a domed nest, which as a rule resembles a great boss of bright green moss. The domicile of the wren is simply a small edition of the last, and often contains as many as seven or eight eggs. A curious habit may frequently be observed in connection with the wren's nesting, that of beginning several structures and then abandoning them. Nests, too, are not unfrequently built and occupied in winter, quite a colony of wrens at this time huddling together for the sake of warmth. Mr. Weir watched a pair at work building, and found that although the nest was commenced at seven o'clock in the morning it was completed the same night. There can be no question as to the clever adaptation of the wren's nest to its surroundings. When it is built in a mossy bank its exterior is of moss, often with a dead leaf on the outside. A nest which was against a hayrick was composed outwardly of hay; while another, in a raspberry bush, was wholly composed of the leaves of that plant.

Probably the only hang-nests of British birds are those of the gold-crest, reed-warbler, and long-tailed titmouse. The first is usually hung among the long, trailing tassels of the pine, where it is most difficult to detect. It is quite one of the prettiest examples of bird architecture, and is thickly felted with wool, feathers, and spiders' webs. The eggs are white, speckled with red. Montague kept a brood of eight nestlings in his room, when he found that the female bird fed them upon an average thirty-six times an hour, and that this was continued sixteen hours a day. Besides being built in pines, the nests are sometimes attached to yews and cedars. The cradle of the reed-warbler is invariably hung upon the stalks of reeds, rushes, and other aquatic plants; and the whole structure is often swayed about so much by the wind as not unfrequently to touch the water. The bottle-shaped nest of the long-tailed tit is almost as remarkable as its builder. It is exquisite alike in form and material, and its interior is a perfect mass of feathers. In one nest alone were found two thousand three hundred and seventy-nine, chiefly those of the pheasant, wood-pigeon, rook, and partridge. Sometimes a great many eggs are found in the nest of the long-tailed titmouse—as many as twenty, it is stated —and these are white, speckled, and streaked with red.

The colours of eggs in relation to birds and the site of their nests is an exceedingly interesting phase of the philosophy of the subject. It is found as an almost invariable rule that birds which lay white eggs nest in holes as a means of protection. The high-flying, loud-screeching swift is an instance of this. So is the burrowing sand-martin, the kingfisher, the shell-duck, and the woodpecker; also the puffin and the stock-dove, which breed in disused rabbit burrows. All these lay white eggs.

The hole which the swift selects is usually in a high building; while the delicate bank-swallows drill their holes in river banks or sandholes. The eggs of the kingfisher are perhaps the most beautiful of all. They are beautifully round, delicately white, glossy, and suffused with an exquisite rosy flush. For breeding, the kingfisher either drills a hole for itself or occupies that deserted by some small rodent. The seven or eight eggs are placed at the end of the burrow, upon a mass of dry fish bones ejected by the bird. The nest is so friable that it is almost impossible to remove it, and at one time it was said that the authorities at the British Museum were prepared to pay one hundred pounds for an absolutely perfect nest of the kingfisher.

The sheld is the largest and handsomest of British ducks. It invariably breeds in a burrow on a plateau commanding the sea, and when approaching its nest plumps right down at the mouth of the hole. Its creamy eggs are large and round; and for a day or so after the young are hatched they are kept underground. Emerging from their retreat, they are immediately led or carried down to the tide. The young seem to be able to smell salt water, and will cover miles to gain it. An interesting fact anent another of our British ducks centres about the golden-eye, an exquisite study in black and white, the back of the neck and head being burnished with violet and green. A trait which the golden-eye has is its almost invariable habit of nesting in holes in trees—remarkable in the case of a duck—so that the Laps place darkened boxes by the sides of rivers and lakes for the ducks to lay in. Often as many as a dozen eggs are found, and the nests are lined with the soft down of the birds. The golden-eye has been seen to transport its young to the water from a considerable altitude. While botanising by the side of a lake, where these beautiful birds breed in great numbers, a Lap clergyman observed one of them drop into the water, and at the same time an infant duck appeared. After watching awhile and seeing the old bird fly to and from the nest several times, he made out that the young bird was held under the bill, but supported by the neck of the parent.

All the British woodpeckers bear out the theory already stated. They lay glossy white eggs, and their nests, (if the touchwood upon which their eggs are deposited can be so called,) are always built in holes in growing wood or decayed timber. The stock-dove, one of our pretty wild pigeons, nests in colonies in rabbit-burrows, as does the brown owl. When ferreting for rabbits the writer has put both these birds out of the holes instead of their rightful owners. The nuthatch is yet another bird which upholds the same rule, and whose case is peculiarly interesting. It not only lays purely white eggs in holes in trees, but if the hole for ingress and egress is one whit too large it is plastered up by the industrious bird until it barely admits the body of the clever little architect.

The cuckoo is quite a Bohemian among birds, and it is doubtless owing to its vagrant habits that there yet remain several points in its life-history which have to be cleared up. The most interesting of these questions are those which relate to its nesting and nidification. It was once thought that the cuckoo paired, but it is now known that the species is polygamous. The number of hens that constitute a harem is not known, but from the number of bachelor birds the males must greatly predominate over the females. Dissection conclusively proves that each female lays a series of eggs, and that these occur in the ovary in widely different stages of maturity. The older naturalists thought that the cuckoo laid its eggs actually in the nests of other birds, but it is now known that it conveys them thither in its bill. The egg of the cuckoo has been found in the nests of sixty different species, several of which are exceedingly small, and moreover domed. Among the sixty nests patronised were the unlikely ones of the butcher-bird, jay, and magpie—all either bird or egg destroyers. This may seem to reflect on the cuckoo's stupidity; and the bird certainly exhibits deplorable ignorance of the fitness of things when it deposits its egg in the nest of the diminutive goldcrest or the cumbersome one of the cushat. A goldcrest might conveniently be stowed away in the gape of a young cuckoo without the latter detecting that the morsel was much more than a normal supply. The nests in which the eggs of cuckoos are most frequently found are those of the meadow-pipit, hedge-sparrow, and reed-warbler. Now the eggs of these birds vary to a very considerable degree; and the question arises whether the cuckoo has the power of assimilating the colour of its egg to those among which it is to be deposited. Certain eminent continental ornithologists claim that this is so, but facts observed in England hardly bear out the conclusion. Brown eggs have been found among the blue ones of the hedge-sparrow, redstart, wheatear; among the green and grey ones of other birds; and the purely white ones of the wood-pigeon and turtle-dove. The cuckoo's egg is brown, and it must be admitted that the great majority of the nests which it patronises contain eggs more or less nearly resembling its own. There is a general family likeness about those laid by the bird, not only in the same clutch, but from year to year. Admitting that the eggs of the cuckoo as a species vary more than those of other birds, it is yet probable that the same female invariably lays eggs of one colour. This can only be surmised by analogy, though the one fact bearing on the question is where two cuckoo's eggs were found in the same nest, and which differed greatly. More might have been learnt from the incident had it been known for certain whether the eggs were laid by the same or different birds. There is a general tendency in the habits of animals to become hereditary, and it seems not unreasonable to suppose that a cuckoo which has once laid its egg in the nest of any particular species should continue to do so, and that its offspring also should continue the practice in after years. A possibility with regard to the cuckoo is that it is not so destitute of maternal instinct as is generally supposed, and that it occasionally hatches its own eggs. It is certain that a female has been seen with her breast destitute of feathers, and with young cuckoos following her and clamouring to be fed. Some other species of the genus nearly akin to our own bird are quite normal in their nesting habits, and I here suggest that, under certain circumstances, our English cuckoo may be so likewise.

The dotterel is one of the most interesting of British birds. It is a summer visitant, and breeds upon the tops of the highest mountains. It is every year decreasing as a species in consequence of the persistency with which it is hunted down for its feathers; these are used for dressing flies. I have found it breeding upon Skiddaw, Sca Fell, and Helvellyn, though not since the year 1884. Part of the interest which attaches to the bird arises from the fact of its extremely local distribution, the mountains named being perhaps the only ones on which it is known to breed in this country. Hewitson, the eminent ornithologist, spent five consecutive seasons in looking for a dotterel's nest; and it was upon Great Robinson and the Hindsgarth range that he ultimately found its eggs. The large price offered for these has acted as a prize for the dotterel's extermination by the shepherds; and some years ago a quarryman had a dog which was trained to find the nests. Owing to the great number of trout streams in the Lake district, angling is general; and, as has been said, the dotterel's decrease is due entirely to the great demand for skins. The birds are mainly shot either on their spring or autumnal migration, and at the former season the grandfather of the present writer upon one occasion bagged seventeen birds in a morning.

Although eagles are now more than rare in Britain, there was a time when they bred among the crags of Cumbria. Gray and Sir Humphrey Davy watched the eagles in their eyries, and the former tells how he saw them robbed of their young. To say nothing of the carnage made on hares, grouse, and waterfowl, these birds during the breeding season destroyed a lamb daily. It is no wonder that the farmers, shepherds, and dalesfolk were careful to plunder the eyries, though this was not done without very considerable risk. In one case a man was lowered down the rocks a distance of fifty fathoms, and during the descent he had to protect himself against the attacks of the parent birds. Year by year the eggs or eaglets were taken, and as their presence was injurious to the interests of the farmers, the latter were willing to pay for their extermination. If the nest contained young birds, these were to be the cliff-climber's remuneration; but if eggs, every neighbouring farmer paid for each egg five shillings. The nests were formed of the branches of trees, and lined with coarse grass and bents that grew on the neighbouring rocks. On the eagles being so frequently robbed of their young, they became unsettled and removed from crag to crag. On one mighty escarpment more inaccessible than the rest they nested for fourteen consecutive years. These eagles and their progenitors had probably bred in the near vicinity for centuries; and the conservatism of birds—especially birds of prey—is quite remarkable. Of this two instances may be given. In *Cotheca Wolleyana* it is recorded that a peregrine falcon's nest on a hill called Arasaxa, in Finland, is mentioned by the French astronomer Maupertius as having been observed by him in 1736. In 1799 it was rediscovered by Skjöldebrand and Acerti. Wolley himself found it tenanted in 1853, and by examining the remains of a young bird lying near the nest, proved that it belonged to this species. It is probable, therefore, that this particular eyrie had been used by the same species of falcon for one hundred and seventeen years.

The following is another instance, hardly less remarkable, though having reference to an altogether different kind of bird. The particular incident is well known to naturalists, and perhaps the latest rendering of it is that by the Nestor of British ornithology, Professor Newton. He says: "When the blue titmouse has taken possession of a hole, she is not easily induced to quit it, but defends her nest and eggs with great courage and pertinacity, puffing out her feathers, hissing like a snake, and trying to repel the fingers of the intruder. . . . . The branch containing the nest may even be sawn off and conveyed to a distance (a cruel experiment) without the mother leaving it, and cases have been known in which, when this has been done, she has still continued to sit on her eggs, hatch them, and rear her brood. With equal persistence will this species year after year use as a nursery the same hole, and a remarkable instance of this kind is on record. In 1779, according to one account, in 1785, according to another, it is said that a pair of these birds built their nest in a large earthenware bottle which had been left to drain in the branches of a tree in a garden at Oxbridge, in the township of Hartburn, near Stockton-on-Tees, and safely hatched their young. The bottle having been allowed to remain in the same position by the occupiers of the farm, then and still [a family of the name of Callendar, was frequented for the same purpose and with a like result, until 1822, when, the tree becoming decayed, the bottle was placed in one near by, and the tenancy continued until 1851. In that year the occupiers of the farm omitted drawing out the old nest, as had been the constant practice before the breeding season, and in consequence the birds chose another place; but in 1852 they returned to the bottle, and have annually built in it, or in a second bottle, which has lately been placed close by it, up to the present year, 1873, with the exception of one season, when a pair of great titmice took possession of their inheritance. The intruders were shot, and the tenancy, it is hoped, will not be again disturbed."

Many birds show that they have the power of not only cleverly adapting themselves to circumstances in matters concerning their nesting, but that they are also equal to unforeseen accidents, which not unfrequently occur. From the secluded haunts and hideling habits of birds of the rail kind, it would hardly be imagined that they were endowed with much intelligence. Here is a striking instance, however, to the contrary. A pair of waterhens built their nest upon an ornamental piece of water of considerable extent, which was ordinarily fed from a spring, and into which another large pond was occasionally emptied. This upon one occasion was done while the female was sitting, and, as the nest had been built at low water, the sudden influx from the second pond caused the water to rise so rapidly as to threaten the destruction of the eggs. This the birds seemed aware of, and immediately took precautions against it. The gardener on the estate, knowing of the sudden rise of water, went to look after the nest, though quite expecting to find the eggs ruined. Instead of this he saw both birds busily engaged about the nest, and adding, with all possible despatch, fresh materials to the fabric to bring it above the impending flood. This they not only succeeded in doing, but it was observed that upon the first rush of water they had removed the eggs to a distance of some feet from the margin of the pool. In the meantime the nest rose rapidly in height, and when the water began to retire the eggs were brought back and placed in the nest. In a few days these were hatched, and the young were swimming with their parents about the pool. The nest plainly showed the formation of the old and new material, and testified to the instinct or reason of the bird architects. In this connection birds have been known to adapt their nests to changed forms of architecture; and almost innumerable little devices may be seen in individual nests tending to their special safety or protection. As an instance of adaptation to haunt it may be mentioned that in the north, buzzards and ravens invariably nest among the rocks of the crags, whilst in the south their nests are just as invariably found in trees.

Both the eggs and plumage of game birds offer interesting instances of this adaptation. The pencilled plumage of the snipe lying still in the brown marshes it is impossible to detect, although the birds get up at one's feet everywhere. The same may be said of the woodcock in the leaf-strewn woods, and of the nests and eggs of both species. The eggs of the wild-duck assimilate to the colour of the green reeds, and those of the lapwing to the ploughed field or the upland. The colour of the red grouse conforms very nearly to that of the purple heather among which it lies, as do the richly-speckled eggs. The partridge has a double protection. It is difficult to pick out her quiet brown plumage from a hedge-bottom so long as she remains still. She adopts the duns and browns and yellows of the dead leaves, among which she crouches. When she leaves her eggs she is careful to cover them with dead oak-leaves; but this seems almost superfluous, for there is no great contrast between the tint of the eggs and that of the leaves among which they lie. A hen pheasant lying in a bracken-bed is equally difficult to detect; and this applies particularly to all the young of the game birds just mentioned. The bright, dark eyes of birds and animals frequently betray them, as these are almost invariably large and prominent. A short-eared owl on a peat-moss I have mistaken for a clod of turf, and a gaunt heron with wind-fluttered feathers for drift stuff caught in the swaying branches of the stream. Another characteristic case of protective imitation is furnished by the nightjar or goatsucker. This night-flying bird, half owl, half swallow, rests during the day on bare bits of limestone on the fells. Its mottled plumage exactly corresponds with the grey of the stones, and its eggs, in colour like its plumage, are laid upon the bare ground without the slightest vestige of a nest— and again entirely resemble the stone.

It will be remarked that all the birds mentioned live much upon the ground, obtaining the principal part of their food therefrom, and that therefore they have need of special protection. Incubation in every case takes place on the ground; and just as the imitation of the plumage of the female bird is perfect, so will the fact tell upon the survival of the species. There is no such need of protection for tree builders, as these, for the most part, are out of the way of predatory animals. The chaffinch is by far the most abundant bird of our fields and woods; and there is one good reason why it should be so. It invariably covers its nest on the outside with dead lichens, like to those of the trunk against which it is built. Against boys and other predatory creatures the device succeeds admirably, and the chaffinch as a species flourishes vigorously. The wren constructs her nest of moss, placing it upon a mossy background so as to present no sharp contrasts. Sometimes she interweaves one or two dead oak-leaves, so as to render the deception more deceitful; and, from the number of wrens which abound, she evidently succeeds. Starlings and sparrows and jackdaws, which build in holes at a considerable elevation, and have therefore less need of protection, hang out straws and sticks and bits of wool and feather as impudent advertisements. Wheatears and such birds as build in low walls cannot afford to do this, but instead build neat nests leaving no trace without. Several of our leaf-warblers drag dead leaves to the outside of their nests, and a hundred others employ like ingenuities.

With regard to sexual colour, the dull summer plumage which characterises so many ground-breeding birds is all the more remarkable as they are the mates of males for the most part distinguished by unusual brilliancy. The few exceptions to this rule are of the most interesting character, and go eminently to prove it. In these exceptions it happens that the female birds are more brightly plumaged than the males. But in nearly the whole of the cases this remarkable trait comes out—that the male actually sits upon the eggs. Now this fact more than any other would seem to indicate that the protection afforded by obscure colouring is directly intended to secure the bird's safety during the most critical period of its life-history. And it has been seen that the law of protective colouring most influences those birds which breed on the ground. One remarkable instance of this may be given, that of the dotterel, a bird already mentioned. This is a species of our own avi-fauna, one which breeds on the summits of the highest mountains. Mr. Gould has remarked that dotterel have not unfrequently been shot during the breeding season with the breast bare of feathers, caused by sitting on the eggs; and the writer knows of his personal knowledge that the shepherds on the Cumbrian mountains occasionally kill dotterel on the actual nest, and that these almost invariably turn out to be males. In winter the colouring of the sexes is almost identical; but when the breeding season comes round the female dons a well-defined, conspicuous plumage, while it is found that the dull-coloured male alone sits upon the eggs. Mr. Wallace has pointed out that bee-eaters, motmots, and toucans—among the most brilliant of tropical birds—all build in holes in trees. In each of these cases there is but little difference in the plumage of the sexes, and where this is so the above rule is almost invariable. Again, our native kingfisher affords an illustration. The orange-plumaged orioles have pensile nests, which is a characteristic of the order to which they belong, most of the members of which are conspicuous. Bird enemies come from above rather than below, and it will be seen that the modifications referred to all have reference to the upper plumage.

In 1888 an egg of a great auk was sold for one hundred and sixty guineas, whilst more recently an egg of the same species fetched two hundred and twenty-five pounds; and although these may seem enormous sums to give for a relic, the transactions are not without others to keep them in countenance. Only a few years ago two eggs of the same kind fetched one hundred and one hundred and two guineas respectively; while the egg first named realised thirty-three pounds ten shillings a little over twenty years ago. At that time it was discovered, together with four others, packed away in a dust-covered box in the museum of the Royal College of Surgeons, these being sold in 1865. From this it would seem that in the ornithological market the complete shell of a great auk's egg is worth nearly one hundred and seventy pounds, and a broken one only seventy pounds less. It will be seen that the purchase of one of these may be a good investment; and what a mine of wealth a great auk that was a good layer might prove to its fortunate possessor can only be conjectured. At the present time the number of eggs of this species known to exist is sixty-six, twenty-five of which are in museums and forty-one in private collections. Of the total number forty-three are retained in Great Britain. When a bird becomes so rare that the individual remains can be counted, the same may be taken to be practically extinct as a species. The great auk has pursued a policy of extinction for the past two or three centuries, until now, like the mighty moa and the dodo, it has ceased to exist. The great auk, or gare-fowl, was one of those birds which, from long disuse, had lost at once the power of flight and preservation. It was a great shambling bird, as large as a goose, and ill adapted to travel on land. How these things told against it may be inferred from the story of one Captain Richard Whitbourne, who writing of the discovery of Newfoundland in 1620, says that among the abundant water-fowl of these parts are penguins (great auks) "as bigge as geese, and flye not, for they have but a short wing, and they multiply so infinitely, upon a certain flat island, that men drive them from thence upon a boord, into their boats by hundreds at a time." This process of extinction went on in Iceland and elsewhere until about the middle of the present century hardly any birds remained. The Icelanders robbed the auks of their eggs for domestic use, and upon one occasion the crew of a British privateer remained upon one of the skerries all day killing many birds and treading down their eggs and young. This went on until the last birds were taken, and there is but the faintest hope that it may yet linger on in the inaccessible North. Although awkward, and travelling with the greatest difficulty on land, the great auk was perfectly at home in the water, and travelled both upon and under the surface with the rapidity of a fish. The time of haunting the land was during the breeding season, in early summer. At this period the auk resorted to the rocks, in the dark recesses of which the females deposited one large egg—large even for the size of the bird. These had a whitish-green ground, streaked with brown, and nearly five inches in length.

CHAPTER VIII.

MINOR BRITISH GAME BIRDS.

AT the time of the heaviest bird migrations in autumn, vast flocks of woodcocks pitch on the English coasts. They stay through the winter, and in spring the majority again cross the wild North Sea *en route* to their northern breeding haunts. The woodcock is a "shifting" species, and just as any bird is erratic in its wanderings, so it is interesting to naturalists. The British Association is already on the track of the "woodsnipe," as are several individual observers in a more literal sense. There was a time when the nesting of the woodcock in England was of such rare occurrence as to be recorded in the natural history journals. We now know that it has bred in almost every English county, and that the number of birds which remain in our woods to breed is annually increasing. This fact proves that the woodcock's habits are being modified, and ornithologists have now to discover the reasons of its extended range.

In coming to this country, woodcocks generally travel in the night and against a head-wind. Those which are exhausted pitch upon the east coast, and here lie resting until nightfall, when they pass on. The probability is that if these birds had not experienced a rough passage they would not have touched the eastern seaboard, but would have kept well in the upper currents of the air, and first dropped down in our western woods or even those of Ireland. The migratory bodies are usually preceded by flocks of tiny goldcrests; and so invariable is this rule that the latter have come to be called "woodcock-pilots." The males precede the females by a few days; the latter bringing with them the young that have been bred that year. It is a point worthy of notice, and one upon which much confusion exists, that the birds that come to us are usually in the very best condition. Soon after their arrival they disperse themselves over the leaf-strewn woods, the same birds being known to resort to the same spots for many successive years. They seek out the warmer parts of the wood, and in such secluded situations sleep and rest during the day. At dusk they issue forth in their peculiar owl-like flight, to seek their feeding grounds. Like many birds they have well-defined routes, and daily at twilight may be seen flying along the rides and paths of the woods or skirting along certain portions of plantations. Coppice-belts they like best, especially such as contain spring-runs. It is here that the bird most easily finds food, the soft ground enabling it to probe quickly and to a considerable depth in search of earthworms. These constitute its principal diet, and the quantity that a single bird will devour is enormous. The long mobile bill of the woodcock is a study in itself. The rapidity with which the bird uses it in following a worm in the ground is marvellous. It is extremely flexible —so much so as to be bent and twisted into every shape without suffering harm—and it is as sensitive as flexible.

Every sportsman knows that woodcocks are here to-day, gone to-morrow. He often finds that where there were plenty yesterday not a single 'cock remains. Ireland, perhaps, affords the best shooting. It was here that the Earl of Clermont shot fifty brace in one day. This feat was the result of a wager; and the bag was made by two o'clock in the afternoon, with a single-barrelled flint-lock. The birds were shot in a moist wood; and it is in such spots on the mild west coast that the woodcock finds its favourite haunt. In England the birds affect coppice-woods, frequenting most those which are wet, and such as have rich deposits of dead and decaying leaves. Most of these copses are of oak and birch and hazel, and being only of a few

L

years' growth are thick in the top. Killing 'cock, as they dash through the twigs of these and seldom rising above the bushes, is one great test of a shooter's skill. Then the birds have a habit of dropping down at a short distance, which almost invariably deludes the inexperienced gunner. When they are put up from their resting places during the day the flight is rapid ; at evening it is slow. It is now that they are easiest to shoot ; though in some parts of the country they are still taken in nets as they fly at dusk through the paths of the woods. Netting woodcocks was at one time the common way of taking them ; for they have always been highly esteemed as food. Another method of capture was by "gins" and "springs ;" and it would seem that in times past the "woodsnipe" was considered a stupid bird. None of the denizens of the woods conforms better or more closely to its environment. The browns and duns and yellows of its plumage all have their counterpart in the leaves among which it lies ; and it has been pointed out that the one conspicuous ornament of the bird is covered by a special provision from the gaze of those for whose admiration it is not intended. This is the bright colouring of the tail feathers, which cannot be seen except at the will of the bird or in flight. Its protection lacks in one thing, however, and that is its large dark eye ; this is full, bright, and (so to speak) obtrusive. It is not often that a special provision of this kind is injurious to its owner; but the lustre which beams from the woodcock's eye is apt to betray its presence, and even to negative the advantage of its protective colouring. This has long been known. Hudibras has it that :

> " Fools are known by looking wise,
> As men find woodcocks by their eyes."

The woodcock is an early breeder, the eggs being found by the second week in March. These are usually four in number; and the nest is placed among dry grass, leaves, and fern. The young are able to run immediately they are hatched, and are sometimes found with portions of shell adhering to their down. In a few days they are led to the vicinity of water, where they remain until they are able to fly. It is said that a small bank of moss is sometimes constructed by the old birds, upon which worms are placed. In its yielding substance they have their first lesson in boring, and obtain the kind of food which constitutes their chief diet in after life. One of the most interesting traits about the woodcock is the fact of its occasionally conveying its young through the air; which is done by only one or two other birds. This is no recent discovery. The fact was known as early as the middle of last century;

though Gilbert White rightly surmised that those observers were mistaken who fancied the young were conveyed either by or in the bill. It is just as erroneous, however, to substitute the claws, as some have done, for the bill. The truth is, that when the parent bird wishes to convey her young one from a place of danger to one of safety, the tiny thing is gently pressed between the feet and against the breast, the aid of the bill being resorted to only when the burden has been hastily taken up. In this way the whole of the brood is sometimes removed from one part of a wood to another, if the birds have been much disturbed. This trait may be confirmed by any one who will look out the bird in its haunts, and is all the more interesting as it seems to be quite an acquired one. The bird is in no way adapted to transport its young through the air.

There are upwards of a dozen species of British plover; birds interesting to the naturalist, dear to the heart of the shore-shooter and to the sportsman of the marshes. Some of these are summer visitants to our shores, others come in winter, while a few stay with us throughout the year. The common green plover or peewit, with its crest, its peculiarly rounded wings, its plaintive cry, is the best known; and this species breeds with us, as the abundance of its eggs shows. In autumn the old birds and their young descend from the uplands where the latter are bred, and seek out the mud-banks and ooze-flats on which to spend the winter. Plashy meadows and marshes are also favourite feeding grounds; and here the lapwing makes "game" for an army of gunners. The vast flocks of plovers that congregate in autumn are said to be growing in numbers. Hundreds of thousands of eggs are collected annually; bunches of green plover are displayed at the gameshops during the autumn; and yet there are more of these birds in England than ever there were. This may be accounted for by the closeness with which the plover conforms to its environment through every season. The plover is dainty eating, as are also its eggs. "To live like a plover"—meaning to live on the wind—is a saying of no aptitude. All the species are voracious feeders on substantials. Their chief food consists of insects and worms from ploughed land; but immediately upon the setting in of frost they betake themselves to the mosses and marshes, or even to the coast and estuaries of rivers. Here they feed liberally and at large, becoming plump and fat. On these grounds the birds often remain till the return of spring. Although many are shot, most of the birds that find their way to market are taken in nets by professional fowlers. When the flocks are heaviest, and during hard weather, from fifty to eighty plovers are sometimes secured at one raising of the net.

Flying with the lapwing may often be seen flocks or "trips" of golden plover—one of the most beautiful birds of its family, and much less common as a species than the last. Like the rare dotterel it breeds on the highest mountains, and in the nesting season has the golden markings of its back set off by the rich velvety black of its breast. This is an adornment donned only for the summer season, and is changed at the time of the autumnal migration from the elevated breeding grounds to the lowlands. At all times it has a piping, plaintive whistle, which conforms well to the wild solitudes where it is heard. The flocks of golden plover are usually smaller than those of green, and are more compact. When feeding together the two kinds are not easily discriminated. The moment they take wing, however, a difference is detected; the golden plover flying straight and quick, often in a V-shaped bunch; the green going loosely and without apparent order. All plover are restless and shifting before a change of weather, and when this is for the worse the golden plover always fly south. They are delicate birds, in fact, and little fitted to withstand the rigours of our northern climate. As a table bird it is more dainty even than the green plover, and fetches a higher price. The death-dealing punt-gun is terribly destructive to this species, from the compact mode of flying described above. As many as a hundred birds have been killed at a single shot.

The beautiful little ringed plover, or sea-lark, is another of our breeding species. It is permanently resident on our coasts, and is one of the most interesting of British shore-birds. At no time infrequent, there is a considerable accession in winter; and it is a pretty sight to watch a flock of these feeding among sand or shingle, or even upon a mud-flat. It is in such spots, too, that it lays its creamy-spotted eggs (pointed like those of all plovers), often without the slightest semblance of a nest. No shore bird is as nimble as the ringed plover. It runs with the utmost grace and ease, picking up tiny crustaceans as it goes. Although not uncommon, the ringed plover is somewhat locally distributed, which may also be said of the Kentish plover. This is a rare species, and is very seldom found in numbers far from the south-eastern counties—from the saltings of Essex and Kent. In haunt and habit it much resembles the "sea-lark."

Only one other shore bird is resident with us throughout the year; this is the oyster-catcher. Sea-pie and olive it is also called on some parts of our coasts. It is easily distinguished by its well-defined black and white markings, and every shore-shooter knows its shrill rattling whistle, its short uneasy flights, and its restless paddlings up and down the ooze. Watch the sea-pie from behind some boulder and see how admirably adapted is its bill to its wants. Flattened sideways and as hard as stone, no bivalve can resist it. It breeds among the weed and driftwood just above high-water mark, and lays three or four eggs of a cream-coloured ground, blotched and spotted with varying shades of rich dark brown.

The little ringed plover is an exceedingly rare British bird, and is like our own ringed plover in miniature.

The grey plover and the turnstone are spring and autumn visitors, having their breeding haunts in the far north, though it is probable that the first has bred a few times within the British Islands. Specimens have been seen in the London markets attired in summer plumage, and the birds themselves have been observed about the Farne Islands in June. The grey plover is fairly numerous after its advent in September, keeping in small flocks and sticking closely to the coast lines. It is larger than the green and golden plovers, is sometimes seen in company with them, and like them assumes a black breast in the breeding season. It occurs less frequently in the bags of the puntsman than the birds just named; it is rarely obtained far inland. Like its congeners it forms a delicate morsel to the *gourmet*. The turnstone, also known as the Hebridal sandpiper, is a handsome bird in black, white, and chestnnt. In its haunts it feeds upon various sea and sand haunting creatures, which it obtains by turning over the stones with its bill. In this office the birds often assist each other. It comes in September in limited numbers, going north to its breeding haunts early in spring.

The dotterel and Norfolk plover are summer visitants. The former breeds upon the tops of the highest mountains, and rarely stays more than a few days during the times of the spring and autumn migrations. It is every year decreasing in consequence of the persistency with which it is hunted down for feathers for dressing flies. We have found it breeding upon Skiddaw, Sca Fell, and Helvellyn. The Norfolk plover, thick knee, or stone curlew, is a summer visitant, coming in small numbers, and being only locally distributed. It breeds in a few of the eastern counties.

December, with its frost and snow, its cold grey skies, and biting northern weather, always brings with it skeins of swans, geese, and wild-fowl. The heart of the fowler warms as he hears the clangour and wild cries of the birds afar up, for although he cannot see their forms, he easily determines the species. He hears the gaggle of geese, the trumpetings of wild swans, and the cry of the curlew as it hovers over the lights. Among the fowl that are driven down by stress of weather are wisps of snipe, and, although comparatively small, no game is dearer to the heart of the inland sportsman or shore-shooter. Four species of snipe are found in Britain, though one of these, the red-breasted or brown snipe, can only be looked upon as a rare straggler. The remaining three species are the common snipe, the great snipe, and the jack snipe. All snipe have a peculiar zig-zag flight, and this peculiarity renders them most difficult to kill. Bagging the first snipe constitutes an era in life of every sportsman, and is an event always remembered. Another characteristic of birds of this genus is the beauty and design of their plumage. The ground colour is streaked and pencilled in a remarkable manner with straw-coloured feathers, which enables the bird to conform in a marvellous manner to the bleached stalks of the aquatic herbage which constitutes its haunt. The arrangement is somewhat similar to that of the woodcock lying among its dead oak-leaves.

The common snipe is one of our well-known marsh birds, although drainage and better farming have not only restricted its breeding haunts, but have caused it to be less numerous. Still it probably breeds in every county in England, and our resident birds are augmented in numbers by bands of immigrants which annually winter within our shores. These mostly come from Scandinavia, and soon after their arrival may be seen dispersing themselves over the marshes in search of food. At this time they are exceedingly wary, and the alarm-note of a single bird will put every one up from the marsh. The startled cry of the snipe resembles the syllables "scape, scape," which is often a literal translation of what takes place before the gunner. The bird feeds on plashy meadows, wet moors, by tarns and stream sides, and on mosses which margin the coast. And this being so it is one of the first to be affected by severe weather. If on elevated ground when the frost sets in it immediately betakes itself to the lowlands, and when supplies fail here it soon starves, becoming thin and skeleton-like. Under ordinary circumstances the bird is a ravenous feeder, lays on a thick layer of fat, and is certainly a delicacy. Soon after the turn of the year snipe show an inclination to pair, one of them circling high in the air, and flying round and round over their future nesting site. It is now that they produce a peculiar drumming noise, caused as some say by the rapid action of the wings when making a downward swoop; while others assert that the noise is produced by the stiff tail feathers; others again that it is uttered by the bird itself. This "bleating" much resembles the booming of a large bee, and has given to the bird several expressive provincial names. To many northern shepherds the noise indicates dry weather and frost. The snipe is an early breeder, and in open seasons its beautiful eggs may be found by March or early April. These are laid in a depression among rushes or aquatic herbage, and have a ground colour of greenish olive, blotched with varying shades of brown. Incubation lasts only a fortnight, and the result of this are young which run as soon as they are hatched, and clothed in an exquisite covering of dappled down. The birds strongly object to any intrusion on their breeding haunts, though this presents a capital opportunity of hearing the peculiar sound already referred to. The male will be seen flying high in circles, and whenever he indulges the remarkable action of his wings in his curving descent the sound proceeds from him. Upon being hatched the young are immediately led to water and the protection of thick and dank herbage. Here, too, food is abundant, which for these tiny things consists of the lowest forms of aquatic life. It is interesting to watch snipe boring for food, and it is surprising what hard ground their admirably-adapted long mobile bills can penetrate. This is an exceedingly sensitive organ however, the outer membrane being underlaid by delicate nerve fibre, which infallibly tells the bird when it touches food, although far hidden from sight. The seeds which are sometimes found in birds of the snipe kind have come there not by being eaten, but attached to some glutinous food, and eaten accidentally.

The second species, the great snipe, long remained unknown as a British bird, owing to its being considered only a large variety of the bird above mentioned. Pennant was the first to elevate it to the rank of a species, and, once pointed out, its claim was admitted. The great snipe does not breed in Britain, and those killed here are mostly birds of the year, these occurring from early to late autumn. During a single season the writer shot three examples of this bird; one was flushed from turnips, the other two from a high-lying tussocky pasture—an ideal spot for hares, and for which we were on the look-out. In going away the great snipe is much slower than its common cousin, and is not given to zig-zaging to such an extent. It lies close, flies heavily, and on the wing reminds one very much of the woodcock. Unlike its congeners, it does not soon "plump," but flies straight away. "Solitary snipe" is misleading, as a pair are often found in company; whilst double snipe, woodcock snipe, and little woodcock are each expressive and descriptive. With regard to food and habit, this species has much in common with its congeners. It is usually found on high and dry situations from October to the end of the year, and seems to prefer loose soil to wet marshes, as the former give a greater variety of food. This consists of worms, insects and their larvæ, beetles, tiny land-shells and grit. When in season the birds are loaded with flesh and fat. Only a slight nest is constructed at breeding time, when four eggs are laid; these are olive-green with purplish-brown blotches. The bird is not known to breed with us, though it does in Scandinavia, and here it is sometimes known to tear up the surrounding moss with which to cover its back. This it does for the purpose of concealment, a proceeding which is sometimes practised by the woodcock. The following interesting fact is recorded by two gentlemen who have observed the bird in its breeding grounds. "The great snipe has a *lek* or playing ground, similar to that of some of the grouse tribe, the places of meeting, or *spil-pads*, being frequented by several pairs of birds from dusk to early morning. The male utters a low note resembling *bip, bip, bipbip, bipbiperere, biperere*, varied by a sound like the smacking of a tongue, produced by striking the mandibles smartly and in rapid succession; he then jumps upon a tussock of grass, swelling out his feathers, spreading his tail, drooping his wings in front of the female, and uttering a tremulous *sbirr*. . . . . The males fight by slashing feebly with their wings, but the combat is not of long duration." As the characteristics of the great snipe become known, it will doubtless be recorded as occurring more frequently than it has been in the past. As has been suggested, it is most probable that in a big bag of snipe the rarer species may frequently have been overlooked, especially as the common snipe varies in size, perhaps more than any other bird.

The jack snipe is the smallest British species, and is only a winter visitor to this country. It breeds upon the *tundras* of the far north, and arrives here late in September. Unlike its congeners, it is usually seen singly, and it procures its food in the boggiest situations. It feeds much at dusk both morning and evening, and when satisfied retires a short distance upland, where among dry grass tufts it rests during the day. Its food consists of worms and other soft-bodied creatures; under favourable conditions it lays on much fat, and is considered a delicacy at table. Upon its first coming it makes for wet meadows, plashy uplands, and sea-coast tracts, although the weather regulates the altitude at which the bird is found. If severe frost sets in it leaves the hill-tarns for lower land, and seeks the protection of grass and rushes by the margins of streams. Open weather, however, soon drives it from the valleys. The jack snipe is very local in its likes, and will return again and again to the same spot; in ordinary seasons its numbers are about equal to those of the common snipe. It lies well to the gun, often until almost trodden on, and birds have been known to have been picked up from before the nose of a dog. It is more easily killed than any of its congeners, for although it flies in a zig-zag manner it invariably rises right from the feet of the sportsman. About April the birds congregate for their journey northwards, and there is no authentic record of the species having bred in Britain. Mr. John Wolley, an English naturalist, discovered in Lapland the first known eggs of the jack snipe. And this is how he relates the interesting find : " We had not been many hours in the marsh when I saw a bird get up, and I marked it down. The nest was found. A sight of the eggs, as they lay untouched, raised my expectations to the highest pitch. I went to the spot where I had marked the bird, and put it up again, and again saw it, after a short low flight, drop suddenly into cover. Once more it rose a few feet from where it had settled. I fired, and in a minute had in my hand a true jack snipe, the undoubted parent of the nest of eggs ! In the course of the day and night I found three more nests, and examined the birds of each. One allowed me to touch it with my hand before it rose, and another only got up when my foot was within six inches of it. The nest of the 17th of June, and the two of the 18th of June, were all alike in structure, made loosely of dried pieces of grass and equisetum not at all woven together, with a few old leaves of the dwarf birch, placed in a dry sedgy or grassy spot close to more open swamp."

At one time snipe were commonly taken in "pantles" made of twisted horsehair. These were set about three inches from the ground, and snipe and teal were mostly taken in them. In preparing the snares the fowler trampled a strip of oozy ground, until, in the darkness, it had the appearance of a narrow plash of water. The birds were taken as they went to feed in ground presumably containing food of which they were fond.

CHAPTER IX.

WATER POACHERS.

IF trout streams and salmon rivers are ever more interesting than when the "March-brown" and the May-fly are on, surely it must be when the fish are heading up stream for the spawning grounds. Then the salmon leave the teeming seas and the trout their rich river reaches for the tributary streams. At this time the fish glide through the deep water with as much eagerness as they rushed down the same river as silvery samlets or tiny trout. Maybe they stay for a short time at some well-remembered pool, but the first frosts remind them that they must seek the upper waters. A brown spate rolling down is a potent reminder, and they know that by its aid the rocks and weirs will be more easily passed. If the accustomed waterways are of solid foam the fish get up easily, but the soft spray gives them little hold.

Let us watch them try to surmount the first obstacle; and here, by the White Water rocks it is a silvery sight to see the salmon "run." There is a deafening roar from the waterfall, and the almost impalpable spray constitutes a constant maze of translucent vapour. Ever and anon a big fish throws its steel-blue form many feet above the water, endeavouring to clear the obstacle. Many times it is beaten back, but at last it gains a ledge, and by a concentrated effort manages to throw itself into the still deep water beyond. Instead of leaping, the female fish try to run through the foam and on from stone to stone until a last leap takes them over. Where no passes exist many fish are picked up dead, the majority of these prove to be males, and this preponderance is also noticeable upon the breeding grounds. The spawning redds are selected where the tributaries are clear and pure—where there is bright gravel and an entire absence of sediment. Here the fish settle down to their domestic duties, and their movements seem to be regulated by a dulling stupor. This facilitates observation, but it also assists the poacher in his silent trade. Once settled, the female fish scoops out a hollow in the sheltering gravel, and is closely attended by her lord. Whilst spawning is proceeding, observe with what care he attends her, and in what evolutions he indulges. He rises and falls, now passing over, now under her, and settling first upon this side, then upon that. Observe, too, how he drives off the young unfertile fish which are ever lying in wait to devour the spawn. The eggs are deposited at intervals in the sand, and when the milt has been fertilised the whole is covered over, there to remain until spring. The salmon deposits nearly a thousand eggs for every pound of its live weight, and from the quantity of spawn in some salmon rivers it would seem that nothing which man could do—save pollution—would have any appreciable influence upon the increase of the species. The fecundity of trout is even greater than that of salmon, while a tiny smelt of only two ounces contains upwards of thirty-five thousand eggs, and even these are as nothing compared with the rate of increase of several marine and "coarse" fish. An individual cod has yielded more than six million; a turbot fourteen million; and a twenty-eight pound conger eel fifteen million eggs.

The eggs of salmon are nearly as large as the seed of a garden pea, and those of good trout only slightly less. The ova is of a delicate salmon colour and the cell-walls are semi-transparent—so much so that the embryo shows plainly through. Although delicate in appearance they are elastic and capable of sustaining great pressure, and an egg thrown upon a flat surface will rebound like an india-rubber ball. The economy of the extreme prolificness of the sporting fishes of Britain can best be understood when we come to consider the host of enemies which beset both salmon and trout in the very first stages of their existence. Nature is prolific in her waste, and a whole army of nature's poachers have to be satisfied. So true is this that the yearly yield of the largest salmon-producing river in the kingdom is computed at about the produce of *one female fish* of from fifteen pounds to twenty pounds in weight; the produce of all the rest being lost or wasted. Sometimes a single ill-timed spate will destroy millions of eggs by tearing them from the gravel and laying them bare to a whole host of enemies.* These

* "Sometimes while stealing along in a quiet deep channel but a few yards wide, worn through the rock, or between it and the green bank opposite, the spectator would marvel at the broad expanse of shingle or barren sand. Little would he wonder if, after a week's rain, he sought the same spot, when Tweed was coming down in his might, and every tributary stream, transformed for the nonce into a river, swelled the mighty flood. Then timber trees, sawn wood, dead animals, farming implements, even haystacks would come floating down, and the very channel of the river would be diverted, sometimes never to return to its ancient course. Sad was the havoc occasioned among the embryo spawn; torn from its bed, it would be carried down stream, to be devoured by the trout or the eel, or enemies are in the air, on the land, in the water, and nothing short of an enumeration of them can convey any idea of their numbers and wholesale methods of destruction. In addition to the yearling salmon and trout which for ever haunt the skirts of the spawning grounds, there are always a number of mature unfertile fish which for a part of the year live entirely upon the spawn. An instance of this is recorded by a river watcher on the Thames, who states that while procuring trout ova in a stream at High Wycombe, he observed a pair of trout spawning on a shallow ford, and another just below them devouring the ova as fast as it was deposited by the spawner. The keeper netted the thief, and in its stomach was found upwards of two ounces of solid ova, or about three hundred eggs. Eels particularly root up the gravel beds, and the

---

to perish amid the waste of waters. We felt on these occasions pretty safe. Our principal enemies were dispersed: the gulls sought worms in the ploughed uplands; the kingfisher and the solitary heron flew away to the smaller streams, where the less turbid water permitted them to see their prey. The cold, slimy, cruel eel, alone of all our enemies, was then to be dreaded. Crawling along at the bottom of the water, his flat wicked head pressed against the gravel, so as to escape the force of the stream, the wily beast would insinuate himself into every crevice or corner, where a small fish might have taken shelter, or a drowned worm be lodged, and all was prey to him." *The Autobiography of a Salmon.*

small river lamprey has also been seen busily engaged in the like pursuit. These have a method in going about their depredations that is quite interesting. Small parties of them work together, and by means of their suckers they remove the stones, immediately boring down after the hidden spawn. If a stone be too large for one to lift another will come to its aid, even four or five having been seen to unite their forces. It is a good-sized stone which can resist their efforts, and the mischief they do is considerable. Even water beetles and their larvæ must, on account of their numbers and voracity, come within the reckoning, and among the most destructive of these are water-shrimps and the larvæ of the dragon-fly. Have we not been told that while the loved May-fly is "on," all hours, meats, decencies, and respectabilities must yield to his caprice, so that the pink-spotted trout, rushing from every hover, may be lifted gently from its native stream to gasp away its life among the lush summer grass? But if the gauzy-winged fly is one of the loved likes of the trout, the former has its day, for none of the larvæ of water beetles is so destructive to spawn and fry as this. Pike and coarse fish are equally partial to the same repast, and even salmon and trout devour the young of their own kind. Waterfowl are among the trout-stream poachers, and the swan is a perfect gourmand. My swan and her crew (five cygnets) would dispose of two million five hundred thousand eggs in that time. Some of the best trout streams in the country have been depopulated of fish by these birds, and the Thames as a fishing river is now greatly suffering from the number of swans allowed upon it.* Both wild and domestic ducks are destructive to spawn and almost live

* "One had better throw open his pond or river to all the poachers in the district than indulge in a taste for swans. If any one doubts this, let him row up the Thames from Weybridge to Chertsey, or on to Laleham, during the latter end of the month of April or early in May, and take particular and special notice of what the swans are doing, If he has still any doubt, and likes to kill one or two and cut them open, he will solve his doubts and do a service at the same time; he may be fined for it, but he will certainly suffer for a good action and in a good cause. A swan can and will devour a gallon of fish-spawn every day while the spawn remains unhatched, if he can get it; and it is easily found. I leave the reader to calculate what the few hundreds (I might almost say thousands) on the Thames devour in the course of two or three months. Their greediness and voracity for fish-spawn must be witnessed to be believed. If this were not so, the Thames ought to swarm to excess with fish, whereas it is but poorly supplied. Here is a little calculation. Suppose each swan only to take a quart of spawn per diem, which is a very low average indeed; suppose each quart to contain fifty-thousand eggs (not a tithe of what it does contain). I am not speaking of salmon and trout here, their ova being much larger; suppose only two hundred swans (about a fourth, perhaps, of the number really employed) are at

on the "redds" during the breeding season. We have more than once shot moorhens in autumn with spawn dripping from their bills, and the birds themselves gorged with it. The coot has been charged with the same crime, though as yet guilt has only been brought home to it with regard to coarse fish; and to the silvery bleak it is said to be particularly partial. The grebe or dabchick must be looked upon as an arrant little poacher not only of eggs and fry but of fish in every stage of growth. It is said that a pair of dabchicks will do more harm on a river than a pair of otters, which, however, is perhaps not so terrible as it sounds. Fourteen little grebes fishing about a mile of trout stream, as we have known, is overstepping the balance of nature, and would certainly injure the river; and Mr. Bartlett has stated that a pair of these birds which he kept in confinement cost the Zoological Society a considerable sum in providing small fish for them. Frank Buckland

work at the spawn, and give them only a fortnight for the period of their ravages. Now what is the result we get? Why, a little total of one hundred and forty million. One hundred and forty million of eggs! Suppose only half of those eggs to become fish, and we have a loss of seventy millions of fish every year to the River Thames—a heavy price to pay for the picturesque, particularly when the reality may perhaps be doubled, or trebled, or even quadrupled." Francis Francis.

had a grebe sent to him which had been choked by a bullhead, and the same fate has not unfrequently befallen kingfishers and other aquatic feeders. The vegetarian water-voles may be written down innocent with regard to spawn, or at the worst "not proven." Our British voles are miniature beavers that haunt the water sides and lead a fairy-like existence among the osier-beds and lily-pads. They know but little of winter, and therefore of the spawning season, and their delectable lives are lived on through ever-recurring summers. Until lately naturalists knew but little of the life-history of the voles, and the country folk called them "water-rats" and "field-mice," and knew little beyond except that they tunnelled their meadow-banks. As the little creatures pass from one bank to another they swim fearlessly towards the observer, and when within a few yards of the side suddenly disappear and enter their holes from beneath. Much abuse has been heaped upon the vole for its alleged propensity for destroying ova, but as yet nothing has been proved against it. We have watched scores of these little creatures feeding on the succulent leaves of water-plants, but have never detected them searching the "redds" or taking trout fry. It has been asserted that voles feed upon flesh when opportunity offers, but perhaps we cannot

Water Poachers. 171

better vindicate their general character in this respect than by relating an incident which has occurred annually for some years past. In a quiet pool known to us, a couple of moorhens have annually hatched and reared one or more broods under the shadow of an old thorn-tree, the nest being interwoven with one of the lower boughs which floats on the surface of the water. Under the roots a pair of voles have annualy brought forth several young families; and yet perfect amity seems to exist between the birds and the rodents. We have seen the eggs lying for hours uncovered and unprotected, and at other times the young birds, not more than a few hours old, swimming about in the water when the voles were constantly feeding, crossing and recrossing from bank to bank. If voles were addicted to killing birds the downy young of the moorhen would have afforded tender morsels, and have been easily obtained in a small confined pool ere they were able to take wing.

When the eggs of salmon and trout have been submitted to the action of clear running water for a few months they begin to hatch. Prior to this the young fish may be seen inside packed away in a most beautiful manner. The embryo increases in bulk until on some warm April day the tiny fish bursts its shell and finds itself in a wide world of waters. Individual eggs may be seen to hatch, and the process is most interesting. First the shell splits at the part corresponding to the back. Then a tiny head with golden eyes appears, and after two or three convulsive waves of his little tail the now useless shells fall from off him. He seems to enjoy the watery element in which he finds himself, for away he swims as fast as his tiny fins and wriggling tail will carry him, round and round in a circle, until presently he sinks down again to the sheltering gravel, for the first time breathing freely by his delicate gills. Every young salmon and trout has a tiny umbilical sac attached, and upon the contents of which it must feed until it has learnt to look out for itself, a period of from six to eight weeks. Frank Buckland has stated that no other animal increases so rapidly at so little cost, and becomes such a valuable article of food as the salmon. At three days old it is nearly two grains in weight; at sixteen months it has increased to two ounces, or four hundred and eighty times its first weight; at twenty months old, after the smolt has been a few months in the sea, it becomes a grilse of eight and a half pounds, having increased sixty-eight times in three or four months; at two and three-quarter years old it becomes a salmon of twelve pounds to fifteen pounds; after which its increased rate of growth has not been satisfactorily ascertained, but by the time it becomes thirty pounds it has increased one hundred and fifteen thousand two hundred times the weight it was at first.

The only parts of a young salmon or trout which is fully developed immediately it leaves the egg are its eyes. These are golden with a silver sheen, and beautifully bright—the great aids in steering clear of an almost innumerable set of enemies which this new stage of existence brings. And it is really difficult to say whether these game fishes have more enemies when in the egg or after they are hatched. Of some of the former we have already spoken, and now let us look to the latter.

The heron is a great trout-stream poacher, and destroys quantities of immature fish. This has long been known, but the fact received striking confirmation from an incident which occurred at the rearing-ponds at Stormontfield. Here a heron was shot as it left off fishing, when it immediately disgorged *fifty fry*. In the trout stream the heron stands looking more like a lump of drift-stuff caught in the bushes than an animate object. Gaunt, consumptive, and sentinel-like, the bird watches with crest depressed, standing upon one leg. At other times it wades cautiously with lowered head and outstretched neck, each step being taken by a foot drawn gently out of the water, and as quietly replaced in advance. Occasionally the wader steps into a deep hole, but this causes not the slightest flurry. The walk is changed into a sort of swimming, and paddling deep in the water until the feet again touch firm ground. Woe to the trout or samlet that comes within range of the heron's terrible pike, for it is at once impaled and gulped down. This impalement is given with great force, and a wounded heron has been known to drive its strong bill right through a stout stick. If a fish is missed a sharp look-out is kept for its line of escape, and a stealthy step made towards it. Should the distance be beyond range of the bird's vision, a few flaps of the wings are tried in the eagerness of pursuit. Nothing from the size of fry to mature fish comes amiss to the heron, and the young whilst still in the nest consume great quantities. Their swallow is insatiable, though sometimes they gaff an individual which is difficult to dispose of. Shooting late one evening in summer we were standing by a stream the banks of which were riddled with the holes of water-voles. It was almost dark, when a large bird flapped slowly over the fields and alighted by the bank. It took its stand, and as we lay low its sketchy form was sharply outlined against the sky. It was a heron; and for an hour among the dank weeds and wet grass we watched it feed. After a prolonged struggle with some object in the water it rose. Just as it did so we fired, and running up to the winged bird were in time to see a live vole which it had disgorged. As an example of "the biter bit," it is related that a heron was seen one evening going to a piece of water to feed; the spot was visited the next morning, when it was discovered that the bird had stuck its beak through the head of an eel, piercing both eyes; the eel thus held had coiled itself so tightly round the neck of the heron as to stop the bird's respiration, and both were dead. Upon another occasion a heron is said to have swallowed a stoat, but in this case also the prey was promptly disgorged. An authoritative statement has been made to the effect that the heron's services in the destruction of pike, coarse fish, rats, and water-beetles may fairly be set off against its depredations in trout-streams. But to this we must dissent; and if a trout stream and a heronry are to flourish in the same neighbourhood, the former must be covered in with netting, especially during the spawning season.

Another bird which is an enemy to both salmon and trout in their fry stage is the black-headed gull. This bird with its laughing cry hovers over the stream and never lets slip an opportunity of snapping up a brown trout or silvery samlet that has left its place of refuge. The late Francis Francis was fully aware of this fact, and he set down both gulls and terns as most notorious offenders. A couple of hundred gulls will devour at least a thousand smolts per day; and the birds may be seen at Loch Lomond travelling to and from Gull Island and the burns all day, each with a trout or parr in its beak. This must have a considerable effect on the future supply of grilse in the Tweed.

As to what part the pretty white-breasted dipper plays in the economy of salmon rivers and trout streams naturalists are by no means agreed. Frank Buckland said that one might as well shoot a swallow skimming over a turnip-field as a dipper over the spawning beds. And this view of the dipper's economy we believe to be the right and justone. Last autumn we had occasion to walk over many miles of trout streams. In these, fish of every size were upon the gravel beds which constitute the spawning "redds." Almost at every turn the white chemisette of the brook bird glinted from some grey stone and went piping before us up stream. As many of these were seen actually rummaging among the pebbles, some few were shot for examination. Although the post-mortems were carefully conducted, no trace in any single instance of the presence of ova of either trout or salmon could be found, but only larvæ of water-haunting insects, roughly representing the four great families of trout-flies. In opposition to the above, however, it must be admitted that individual dippers have been seen with tiny fish in their bills, and even to feed their young ones upon them. Birds in confinement have also been fed upon minnows, but this *penchant* might be an acquired one. It may be asserted, then, that the ouzel has been known to eat fish, but that fish forms no chief portion of his food; and finally, that it would be quite incorrect to describe it as a fish-eating bird, and therefore as an enemy to salmon and trout. The birds will not long stay where the water is slow or logged; they must have the white foam, the torrent, the pebbly reaches, and the shallows. In fact, they could not obtain their food under conditions other than these. The mountain burns abound with various aquatic insects and their larvæ, and in limestone districts in innumerable fresh-water molluscs. As already shown, not only is the ouzel innocent of destroying eggs of salmon and trout, but it is indirectly beneficial to a fishery. It is well known that among the chief enemies to spawn are the larvæ known as caddisworms, that of the dragonfly, May-fly and stone-fly, and also of the various water-beetles. Now all these have been found in the stomach of the dipper, and therefore it must confer a decided benefit on the salmon and trout streams which it haunts.

Of all our British birds none is so beautiful or so secluded in its habits as the kingfisher; and its presence is peculiarly in keeping with the rapid, rocky trout streams which it loves to haunt. Although glowing with metallic lustres, and beautiful in its adaptation and every movement, the kingfisher builds but a careless nest, a loose structure of dry fish bones—the hard indigestible parts of its food which, in common with birds of prey, it has the power of ejecting in pellets by the mouth. Again, let us look out the bird in its haunts. We follow the course of the hazel-fringed stream over a mile of its pebbly reaches; now a dipper flits from a green mossy stone, and a pair of sandpipers start with tremulous wings and skirt the shingle-strewn banks. Among the flags the water-voles gnaw the sweet saccharine aquatic plants, and the water-hens run and hide under the friendly roots of an overhanging thorn. The May-fly is upon the stream, the silvery fresh run fish are all animation, and even the great black trout in the "willow dub" condescends to take a fat blue-bottle that is spinning round and round the pool. Dragon-flies dart hither and thither, bronze fly and bee are upon the wing, and the carpet of grass and flowers is alive with innumerable insects, all busily engaged in fertilising their floral friends, or revelling in nectar, and gilded with golden pollen. The lime-trees are "a murmurous haunt of summer wings," and the breath of summer is on our cheek. Over there is an overhanging, leafless bough and upon it has just alighted a kingfisher. At first its form is motionless, then it assumes more animation, and anon is all eye and ear. Then it falls, hangs for a moment in the air like a kestrel, and returns to its perch. Again it darts with unerring aim and secures something. This is tossed, beaten and broken with a formidable beak, and swallowed head foremost. This process is again and again repeated, and we find that the prey is small fish. From watching an hour we are entranced with the beauty of the fluttering, quivering thing as the sun glints from its green and gold vibrations in mid-air. We gain some estimation, too, of the vast amount of immature fish which a pair of kingfishers and their young must destroy in a single season.*

* "Then the kingfisher, with rufous breast and glorious mantle of blue, would dart like a plummet from his roost, and seize unerringly any little truant which passed within his ken. The appetite of this bird was miraculous; I never saw him satisfied. He would sit for hours on a projecting bough, his body

Later in summer the young brood may be seen with open quivering wings, constantly calling as the parent birds fly up and down stream. Their food consists almost entirely of fish throughout the year, though during the rigour and frosts of winter they betake themselves to the estuaries of tidal rivers, where their food of molluscs and shore-haunting creatures are daily replenished by the tides. Kingfishers are among the most persistent of trout-stream poachers, and as many as eighty of these beautiful birds have been killed in a season on a famous nursery in the midlands. As in the case of the heron, nothing will save the fry from these marauders but covering in the rearing ponds with the finest wire net. However one may wish to protect the kingfisher, there is no denying the fact of its

almost perpendicular, his head thrown back between his shoulders; eyeing with an abstracted air the heavens above or the rocks around him, he seemed intent only upon exhibiting the glorious lustre of his plumage, and the brilliant colours with which his azure back was shaded; but let a careless samlet stray beneath him, and in a twinkling his nonchalant attitude was abandoned. With a turn so quick that the eye could scarce follow it, his tail took the place of his head, and, falling rather than flying, he would seize his victim, toss him once into the air, catch him as he fell, head foremost, and swallow him in a second. This manœuvre he would repeat from morning till night; such a greedy, insatiable little wretch I never saw!"—*The Autobiography of a Salmon.*

Water Poachers. 181

penchant for fish, especially the fry of salmon and trout; the bad habit is bred in him.

The fact of salmon and trout devouring the spawn of their own kind has been already referred to, and unfortunately the practice is continued after the eggs are hatched. The big fish sometimes so terrify the tiny trout and samlets that the latter throw themselves clear out of the water and lay gasping on the pebbles, while the would-be devourer beats about the shallows disappointed at losing his prey. An old "kelt" salmon has been seen to devour fifty of his own progeny for breakfast; and the pike is a greater water-wolf still. This fish has been known to increase at the enormous rate of from eight to ten pounds a year when favourably placed for feeding. So voracious a creature is the pike, and furnished with such digestion, that it will destroy a half-pound trout a day for twelve months—a terrible drain upon any stream. Then it has an all-capacious maw for silvery smolts as they are making their way down to the sea, and of these at certain seasons it devours myriads. Of course pike keep coarse fish nder, which are indirectly injurious to trout, and in this way confer a benefit upon the angler. There is another way in which he is beneficial, and that is as a scavenger. A diseased salmon or trout never lives more than a few minutes in his presence, for he gulps down fish, fungus, and all. In this connection there is one fact which ought not to be overlooked. Of late years disease has played terrible havoc in some of the best rivers in the country. In one of these, known to the writer, scarcely a fish is caught which does not show scars left by the disease—want of tail, partial loss of fins, and white patches where the fungus has previously grown. That numbers of the fish attacked do survive there can be no question; and that the disease may be prevented at the cost of a few fish we have but little doubt. This may be considered a bold assertion; but in these days of artificial rearing, re-stocking, and preservation, anglers and angling associations are apt either to forget or to ignore the balance of nature. Now, nature rarely overlooks an insult. Destroy her appointed instruments and beware of her revenge. That the salmon and trout may live a whole host of stream-haunting creatures are condemned, and that often upon the most insufficient evidence.

The creature against which the angler "breathes hot roarings out" is the otter. But how few fish does the otter really destroy! The evidence to be gathered by those who live along its streams all goes to show that eels and freshwater crayfish form the staple of its food. In search of these, it wanders miles in a night and will

not partake of soft-bodied fish so long as they
can be found. The economy of the otter ought
not to be overlooked in connection with sport
and our fish supply. Probably its increasing rarity
has as much to do with the disease alluded to
as had the extermination of the nobler birds of
prey with the grouse disease. A falcon always
takes the easiest chance at its prey; and an otter
captures the slowest fish. In each case they kill
off the weakest, the most diseased, and thereby
secure the survival of the fittest. Most of the
newspaper paragraphs anent the doings of otters
are mere legendary stories without any foundation in fact. The otter is not a "fish-slicer."
Salmon found upon the rocks with the flesh
bitten from the shoulders are oftener than not
there by agents other than *Lutra*. A great deal
of unnatural history has been written concerning
the "water-dog," mostly by those who have
never had opportunity of studying the otter in
its haunts. That it occasionally destroys fish we
will not deny; but this liking has become
such a stereotyped fact (?) in natural history
that it is glibly repeated, parrot-like, and has
continued so long, that most have come to
accept it. Ask the otter-hunter, the old angler
of the rocky northern streams, the field naturalist
who has many a night stretched his length along
a slab of rock to observe the otter at home—

and each has the same answer. Abundance of otters and plenty of trout exist side by side; and where the fastnesses of the former are impregnable, there disease is foreign to the stream. Many otters, many trout; this is a bit of nature's economy there is no gainsaying. Here is an actual incident. There is a certain reach on a well-known trout stream which is so overgrown with wood and coppice as to render it unfishable. This reach swarms with handsome well-fed trout; and yet far back among the rocky shelves of the river a brood of otters are brought forth annually, have been in fact time out of mind. And yet another incident. Of forty-five dead otters killed in hunting, in two only were there remains of fish food, and this consisted of eels—deadly enemies either to trout stream or salmon river. These forty-five otters, for the most part, were killed before six in the morning, and consequently when their stomachs were most likely to contain traces of what had been taken in their night's fishing.

One of the most curious enemies of our freshwater fishes is a small floating water-weed, the bladderwort. Along its branchlets are a number of small green vesicles or bladders, which, being furnished with minute jaws, seize upon tiny fish, which are assimilated into its substance. This is a subtle poacher, the true character of which has only lately been detected. The bladderwort is a fairly common plant, and no very special interest attached to it ere its fish-eating propensities were discovered. Its tiny vesicles were known to contain air, and the only use of these so far as was known was to keep the plant afloat—a belief, be it remarked, all the more reasonable because many aquatic plants actually have such air receptacles for that very purpose. The tiny bladders attached to the leaves and leaf-stalks are each furnished with a door, the whole acting on the eel-trap principle, entrance being easy but exit impossible. There is nothing very formidable about the delicate green jaws of the vegetable trap, only that any tiny water creature that ventures in to look round out of mere curiosity never by any chance emerges alive. The first time that the bladder-wort was actually caught at its fish-poaching proclivities, so to speak, was by Professor Moseley, of Oxford. He and a friend had, in a large glass bowl, a plant of this species and also a number of young roach just hatched. The murderous plant held several of the tiny fish in its jaws; and upon an experiment being tried in a separate vessel, it was found that a single plant had captured no less than a dozen fish in the space of six hours. One of these was caught by the head, another by the tail, a third by the yolk-sac, and in another instance two bladders had seized the same fish, one holding on at each extremity. In spite of all this tiny ferocity it must be admitted that this little plant poacher is more interesting than dangerous, and so long as it confines its attention to coarse fish neither the salmon-fisher nor trout-angler will concern himself much about its aquatic depredations.

There is one wholesale method of destruction which particularly affects salmon, which cannot be passed over. This is done by almost innumerable nets, and is usually practised at the mouths of rivers and generally without the slightest regard to the economy of the fish supply. And it has been found that as salmon and the means of transit increase, so does the number of destructive nets. Theoretically, legislation is levelled against this wanton destruction, but practically the law is a dead letter. At every tide, in certain seasons, hundreds of thousands of salmon-fry and smolts are sacrificed; and in a certain firth it is recorded how a fisherman in his nets walked, in many places, knee deep in dead smolts, and that the ground for a considerable distance was silvered with their scales. Under these circumstances the samlets sometimes accumulate to such an extent that they have to be carted on to the nearest land and used as manure. This waste of valuable fish food is so great that it can hardly be reckoned, and in future years must tell greatly upon the British yield of salmon. Mill-wheels * and hatches, too, are often great sources of destruction.

Another enemy to salmon and trout is the great black cormorant—a poacher that studies their migratory and local movements, and acts accordingly. It is the habit of this bird to visit small rivers which flow into the sea, especially during the late winter and early spring months. At these seasons the smolts are preparing to come down, and the kelts of salmon and sea trout are assembling in the large pools prior to their return to salt water. A brace of cormorants which were shot at their fishing were found to contain twenty-six and fourteen salmon

---

* "In this neighbourhood I escaped, by pure good fortune, a danger that I afterwards learnt proved fatal to thousands—nay, tens of thousands—of my young companions. The stream had apparently divided, and whilst I followed the course of the right-hand one, the greater number passed down the wider but less rapid left-hand division. Here they speedily encountered a terrific mill-wheel, and, dashing on one side, they found their progress stopped by a small net, which being placed under them, they were landed literally by bushels. My informant, who escaped by passing under the mill-wheel at the imminent risk of being crushed to death, assured me that the bodies of our unlucky brethren were used as manure! And, degrading as the suggestion is, it seems not impossible, for the numbers taken could not be sold or used for food."—*The Autobiography of a Salmon.*

smolts respectively, and a trustworthy water bailiff asserts that he once watched a couple of cormorants hunt and kill a kelt salmon, and that after dragging it ashore they commenced tearing it up, when they were driven off. It was once thought that both the cormorant and heron only ate that which they could swallow whole, but this is now known not to be strictly correct.

And now, finally, we come to the man poacher. Fish poaching is practised none the less for the high preservation and stricter watching which is so characteristic of the times. In outlying country towns with salmon and trout streams in the vicinity it is carried on to an almost incredible extent. There are many men who live by it, and women to whom it constitutes a thriving trade. These know neither times nor seasons, and, like the heron and the kingfisher, poach the whole year round. They provide the chief business of the county police-court, and the great source of profit to the local fish and game dealer. The wary poacher never starts for his fishing grounds without having first secured his customer; and it is surprising with what lax code of morals the provincial public will deal when the silent night worker is one to the bargain. Of course the public always gets cheap fish and fresh fish—so fresh, indeed, that the life has not yet gone out of it. It is a perfectly easy matter to poach fish, and the

Water Poachers. 189

difficulty lies in conveying them into the towns and villages. The poacher never knows but that he may meet some county constable along the unfrequented country roads, and consequently never carries his game upon him. This he secretes in stacks and ricks and disused farm buildings until such times as it may be safely sent for. Country carriers, early morning milk carts, and women are all employed in getting fish into town. In this the women are most successful. Sometimes they may be seen labouring under a heavy load carried in a sack, with faggots and rotten sticks protruding from the mouth; or again with a large basket innocently covered with crisp green cresses which effectually hide the bright silvery fish beneath.

The methods of the fish poacher are many. The chances of success, too, are greatly in his favour, for he works silently and always in the night. He walks abroad during the day and makes mental notes of men and fish. He knows the beats of the watchers, and has the waterside, as it were, by heart. He can work as well in the dark as in the light, and this is essential to his silent trade. During summer and when the water becomes low the fish congregate in deep "dubs." This they do for protection, and if overhung with trees there is always here abundance of food. If a poacher intends to net a "dub" he carefully examines every inch of its bottom beforehand. If it has been thorned, he carefully removes these small thorned bushes with stones attached, and thrown in by the watchers to entangle the poachers' nets and so allow the fish to escape. At night the poacher comes, unrolls his long net on the pebbles, and then commences operations at the bottom of the river reach. The net is dragged by a man at each side, a third wading after to lift it over the stakes, and so preventing the fish from escaping. When the end of the pool is reached the trout are simply drawn out upon the pebbles. This is repeated through the night until half-a-dozen pools are netted, and maybe depopulated of their fish. Netting of this description is a wholesale method of destruction, always supposing that the poachers are allowed their own time. It requires to be done slowly, however, and if alarmed they can do nothing but abandon their net and run. This is necessarily large, and when thoroughly wet is most cumbersome and exceedingly heavy. The capturing of a net stops the depredations of the poachers for a while, as these being large take long to make. For narrow streams pretty much the same method as that indicated above is used, only the net is smaller, and to it are attached two poles. The method of working this is similar to that of the last.

A species of poaching which the older hands rarely go in for is that of poisoning. Chloride of lime is the agent most in use, as it does not injure the edible parts. This is thrown into the river where fish are known to be, and its deadly influence is soon seen. The fish become poisoned and weakened, and soon float belly uppermost. This at once renders them conspicuous, and as they are on the surface of the stream, they are simply lifted out of the water in a landing-net. This is a wholesale and cowardly method, as it frequently poisons the fish for miles down stream; it not only kills the larger fish, but destroys great quantities of immature ones which are wholly unfit for food. Trout which come by their death in this way have the usually pink parts of a dull white, with the eyes and gill-covers of the same colour and covered with a thin white film. This substance, too, is much used in mills on the banks of trout streams, and probably more fish are destroyed by this kind of pollution in a month than the most inveterate poacher will kill in a year.

Throughout summer fish are in season, but the really serious poaching is practised during close time. When spawning, the senses of both salmon and trout seem to become dulled, and they are not at all difficult to approach in the water. The fish seek the higher reaches to spawn, and stay for a considerable time on the pebble beds.

The salmon offer fair marks, and the poacher obtains them by spearing. A pronged instrument is driven into the fleshy shoulders of the fish, and it is hauled out on to the bank. In this way sometimes more fish are obtained in a single night than can be carried away; and when the gang is chased by the watchers the fish have generally to be left behind, as they are difficult things to carry. The flesh of spawning fish is loose and watery, and is most insipid and tasteless. It is, however, sold to the poorest class of people at a few pence per pound. In one outlying village during last close season poached salmon was so common that the cottagers fed their poultry upon it through the whole winter. It is said that several fish were taken each over twenty pounds in weight. Another way of securing salmon and trout from the spawning "redds" is by means of "click-hooks." These are simply large salmon-hooks bound together shaft to shaft and attached to a long cord; a bit of lead balances them and adds weight. These are used in deep rivers, where spearing by wading is impracticable. When a fish is seen the hooks are simply thrown beyond it, and then gently dragged until they come immediately beneath; a sharp "click" usually sends them into the soft under-parts of the fish, which is then drawn out. That natural poacher, the pike, is frequently ridded from trout streams in this fashion. Of course, poaching with click-hooks requires to be done in the light, or by the aid of an artificial one. Lights attract salmon and trout just as they attract birds, and tar brands are frequently used by poachers. Shooting is sometimes resorted to, but for this class of poaching the habits and beats of the water bailiffs require to be accurately known. The method has the advantage of being quick, and a gun in skilful hands and at a short distance may be used without injuring the fleshy parts of the body. That deadly bait, salmon roe, is now rarely used, the method of preparing it having evidently gone out with the old-fashioned poachers, who used it with such deadly effect.

The capture of either poachers or their nets is often difficult to accomplish. The former wind their sinuous way, snake-like, through the wet meadows in approaching the rivers, and their nets are rarely kept at home. These they secrete about farm buildings, in dry ditches, or among the bushes in close proximity to their poaching grounds. Were they kept at home the obtaining of a search warrant by the police or local angling association would always render their custody a critical one. They are sometimes kept in the poachers' houses, though only for a short period when about to be used. At this time the police have found them secreted in the chimney, between the bed and the mattress, or

o

even wound about the portly persons of the poachers' wives. The women are not always simply aiders and abettors, but in poaching, sometimes play a more important rôle. They have frequently been taken red-handed by the watchers. The vocation of these latter is a hard one. They work at night, and require to be most on the alert during rough and wet weather—in the winter, when the fish are spawning. Sometimes they must remain still for hours in freezing clothes; and even in summer they not unfrequently lie all night in dank and wet herbage. They see the night side of nature, and many of them are fairly good naturalists. If a lapwing gets up and screams in the darkness they know how to interpret the sound, as also a hare rushing wildly past. It must be confessed, however, that at all points the fish poacher is cleverer and of readier wit than the river watcher.

CHAPTER X.

WILD DUCKS AND DUCK DECOYING.

THERE is no European country, however fortunately situated, which has so many species of wild-fowl as Britain. This is partly owing to its insular position, and partly to the food-abounding seas which are on every coast. In their primitive condition these islands must have constituted a very paradise for wild-fowl, and we know that the marsh and fen lands of the south-eastern counties were breeding haunts of myriads of fowl not more than two centuries ago. Even now there are nearly thirty species of wild duck which are either resident or annual visitants to our marine and inland waters. Nearly half of these are now known to have bred within the British Isles, the remaining ones coming from the north only at the severity of winter.

Wild ducks divide themselves into two natural groups according to habit and the manner in which they obtain their food. Sportsmen and fowlers refer to those divisions as "surface" and "diving" ducks. Those which comprise the first class feed exclusively upon the surface and inhabit fresh water; the latter are mostly marine forms, and in procuring their food the whole body is submerged. Among the surface-feeding ducks are the shoveller, sheldrake, mallard, pintail, gadwall, garganey, widgeon, and teal; whilst the latter include the tufted duck, scaup, scoter, surf scoter, velvet scoter, pochard, and golden-eye. Other British ducks which would come naturally into one or other of these groups, but are more or less rare, are the eiders, American widgeon, red-crested pochard, smew, the mergansers, and the buffel-headed, long-tailed, ruddy sheld, Steller's western, ferruginous, and harlequin ducks.

From the fact of their resorting to inland waters the surface-feeding ducks are perhaps the best known. All of them are shy, wary birds, and as difficult of approach as to bring down. Nearly all the species which inhabit fresh water feed during the night, and fly off to the hills to rest and sleep during the day. All of them are birds of considerable powers of flight, and an interesting fact in their economy is the power of the males to change their summer plumage so as to resemble that of the females. As this adaptation only takes place during the breeding season it is probably done for protective reasons.

The common mallard or wild duck, and the

teal, being resident breeding birds, are the first to become noticeable in winter, and many thousands are annually taken in the few remaining decoys of this country. The mallard is an exceedingly handsome bird, and one of the largest of its kind. It is an early breeder, and soon after the brown duck begins to sit the male moults the whole of its flight feathers. So sudden and simultaneous is this process that for six weeks in summer the usually handsome drake is quite incapable of flight; and it is probably at this period of its ground existence that the assumption of the duck's plumage is such an aid to protection. The mallard is not strictly a ground builder, as its nest is sometimes at a considerable altitude, nests of a rook and a hawk having been taken advantage of. In such case the young birds are probably brought to the ground in the bill of the old one. To such an extent did the mallard at one time breed among the fens in this country, that it was customary before the young could fly for a number of persons to engage in what was termed a "driving of ducks," when as many as one thousand eight hundred birds have been taken. Although wild and wary under ordinary circumstances, the mallard upon occasion has shown remarkable tameness. In severe weather two hundred birds have assembled upon a pond and accepted oats at not more than an arm's length from the feeder. Under ordinary circumstances the common wild duck feeds upon floating grasses, grain, insects, and worms; a well-grown mallard sometimes weighs three pounds.

The teal is the smallest of the wild ducks, and is an exquisitely-formed and prettily-marked species. It is dear to the fowler as the gourmet, for it is easily decoyed or stalked, and when procured affords delicate eating. Many a time does the heart of the shore-shooter warm as he hears the whistle of a bunch of teal, and sees them drop down like a plummet. They love to haunt the margins of fresh-water streams and lakes, and when put away from these rise rapidly and as though they had been shot from the water. It is only when their inland resorts are hard frozen that they are driven to the sea, and once here every art of the fowler is used in coming up with them. As many as eighty-five and upon another occasion one hundred and six teal have been picked up after a well-directed shot from a punt-gun—the former by Sir Ralph Payne-Gallwey, the latter off the Irish coast. Both shots were at flying birds. The teal is an early breeder, and being resident is among the first of the ducks seen on the decoys, and with the mallard is the species most abundantly taken. It is liable to the same sexual change in the breeding season, and during the time it has young is most affectionate in tending them. An anecdote is related of how a country lad having fallen in with a brood of teal drove them before him to a lodge. The mother teal followed after, keeping close at hand. When the boy had driven them into a little shed within the yard, the old bird, still following, ran in after them, and in spite of there being dogs and men about did net betray the least alarm.

The sheldrake is one of the largest and handsomest of its kind, and although rare as a resident bird, I have frequently found its nest in rabbit burrows on the shores of Morecambe Bay. It is at all times one of the most distinctive of the ducks with its bright and well-defined chestnut and white plumage. The head and neck are black, but this glows with an iridescent green. Naturalists do not consider this a true duck, but from structural modifications as a connecting link between the ducks and geese. It usually breeds on a plateau commanding the sea, and when approaching its nest it plumps right down to the mouth of the hole. Its creamy white eggs are large and round, eight to twelve being usually found in the burrow. For a day or so after the young are hatched they are kept underground, and immediately upon emerging are led down to the tide. I have not unfrequently taken the eggs from the sand-hills and hatched them under hens—a quite successful experiment up to a certain point. The young seem to be able to smell salt water, and will cover miles of land to gain it. If, however, the distance prove impracticable they will surely leave in autumn when the migratory impulse is strong upon them. This instinct is particularly marked in all sea-fowl, and wild swans, geese, and ducks call loudly to their farm cousins as they pass over. There is a great wildness about the clangour and cries of migratory fowl, coming as it does far up in the wintry sky. Reverting to the breeding of the shelduck, the parents have been observed conveying the newly-hatched young to the sea on their backs when the nest has been far inland. In Holland recesses are cut in the dunes and sand-hills so as to encourage the birds to breed, and each morning the nests are visited and the eggs collected. Ordinarily not more than a dozen eggs are laid, but under this system as many as thirty are produced by a single duck. After the 18th of June the persecution ceases and the birds are allowed to hatch in peace. Most of the nests are lined with fine down little inferior in quality to that of the eiders, this too becoming a commercial commodity.

Being driven from their bleak northern haunts by the ice, widgeon appear in immense flocks in winter, and are by far the commonest of the migratory ducks. They first begin to arrive about October, and continue coming until the end of the year. Although found upon inland lochs and rivers, they love to frequent weed or grass-grown ooze and mud-banks, where they sleep and feed. The widgeon is an exception to most of the wild ducks, as it feeds more by day than by night, and, like geese, it is particularly fond of nibbling the short grass on the saltings. It has a wild whistle which resembles the syllable "whew"—by which name the bird is known on many parts of the coast. Sometimes during a lull in a spell of rough weather vast flocks concentrate themselves on the ooze, and it is at this time they are sought by the puntsman or fowler. When good shots have been obtained at such masses of birds over a hundred have been killed at a single shot, and this explains why widgeon are sold so cheaply in the markets. When winter breaks up the flocks retire northward, only a few remaining to breed on the northern parts of Britain. The widgeon is not known to have nested in England.

The shoveller is another handsomely-plumaged duck, and has its name from its shovel-shaped bill, by which characteristic it may be known at a glance. It is a winter visitor to our shores, though not in any great numbers, and breeds not unfrequently in several of the south-eastern counties as well as more sparingly in the north. It rarely frequents the sea, being fond of fresh water, and is remarkable in the fact that it does not reach down like other ducks to procure its food; it rather filters the water through its bill, retaining the solid animal matter, and allowing the rest to filter through two peculiar processes with which it is fitted. It is rather a foul feeder, swims low in the water, and is admirably fitted for its special mode of life.

The gadwall, which has been described as a "thoroughbred" looking duck, is the rarest yet mentioned. It may not unfrequently be passed over, not only on account of its great shyness, but because it so much resembles the common domestic ducks. It is rare, too, as a breeding species, but an experiment tried in Norfolk shows how easily it may be acclimatised. Here, on the South Acre Decoy, a pair of captured birds were pinioned and turned down, until now, these having bred and attracted others, it is computed that between fourteen and fifteen hundred birds are on the water The gadwall affords admirable eating. The garganey or summer teal is the smallest of the wild ducks with one exception. Unlike the rest, it is not a winter visitant, but only comes to us in early spring on its way northward, and again in autumn on its southward journey. It is an active species, swimming and flying quickly. On land it feeds upon water-weeds, frogs, and grain, and at sea upon crustaceans and molluscs. A few of the migratory birds are known to remain and nest in the reed beds in Norfolk, though the great majority seek their northern breeding grounds. Blue-winged teal is a name given to this prettily-marked species, which to those who know its congener is fairly descriptive. The last of the surface-feeding ducks is the pintail, and if this is also described as handsome it is because there are but few of the wild ducks which are not. It is one of the most graceful, too, and owing to the long central tail feathers of the male is sometimes called the sea-pheasant. Although often obtained by fowlers along the coast, it is also found on inland decoys, and feeds upon aquatic plants, insect larva, and molluscs. Its flesh is next in delicacy to that of the teal, and is held in estimation at table. It is much more rare in the northern than in the southern counties, and off the coast of Cornwall thirty-seven birds have been bagged at one shot. The pintail breeds but rarely in England.

We now come to the diving ducks. Speaking generally, the "surface" ducks haunt fresh water; diving ducks the sea. The most prominent of these are the scaup; common, velvet, and surf scoters; the pochard, golden-eye, and tufted duck.

The inland sportsman or decoy-man knows little of the diving ducks. Some of them keep close to land, but for the most part they are at home far out at sea. It is interesting to watch parties of these playing and chasing each other over the crests of the waves, and seeming indifferent to the roughest weather. The three scoters may be met with fifty miles from land in loosely floating flocks of thousands. The common scoter is a winter visitor to our coasts, sometimes coming in such numbers that the waters between the eastern counties and Holland seem covered with them. This also holds good with regard to the west coast, where the scoters arrive in July. They stay for some days on fresh water; but, once launched on their winter haunt, it is not unusual for a single fisherman to take half a cartload in his "dowker" nets in a a morning. The scoter is entirely black; it dives remarkably well, and can remain a long time under water. It feeds upon mussels and other soft bivalves, following the advancing tides shoreward in search of them. These facts the fisherman notes, and works accordingly. He marks where the birds feed, sees their borings and stray feathers, and when the tide has ebbed spreads his nets. These are attached by a peg at each corner, and laid about fifteen inches above the ground. Returning to feed with the tide, the ducks dive head foremost into the nets and become hopelessly fast. Another of the sea-ducks, the scaup, is also taken in large numbers in this way. But, owing to the oily nature of their flesh and its fishy taste, these birds are rarely eaten. It is owing to this fact that during Lent in Catholic countries the flesh of the scoter is allowed to be eaten. Close cousin to the last and somewhat rarer is the velvet scoter, a handsome duck, with velvety black plumage relieved by a purely white patch on the wing and a crescent-shaped spot of the same colour under the eye. This, too, is a winter visitant, enjoying and obtaining its food in the roughest wintry seas. A few velvet scoters may always be seen among the immense flocks of the common kind. In haunt and habit, as well as food, the common and velvet scoters are identical. The surf scoter is the rarest of the three British species, and is intermediate in size between the two last. With black plumage like its congeners, it is characteristically marked by a white spot on the forehead and an elongated white streak down the neck. The roughest seas have no terror to the surf scoter, and it is such an expert diver as to be able to fish at a depth of several fathoms. None of the scoters breed in Britain, but nest in the great Northern marshes.

Another of the well-known marine ducks is the pochard, or dun-bird. To fishermen and fowlers it is known as "poker" and "redhead," owing to the bright chestnut colouring of its head and neck. This, with its black breast and beautifully freckled grey back, make it a handsome bird. It is somewhat heavily made, swims low in the water, and from its legs being placed far behind for diving it is awkward on land. In winter the pochard is abundant on the coast, but it is one of the shyest of fowl and is always difficult of approach. If alarmed it paddles rapidly away, turning its head and keeping its eye on the intruder. As a consequence of its extreme wariness pochards are much more frequently netted than shot. This kind of fowling was mainly practised on flight ponds near the coast, especially in the south-eastern counties. And this is how it was done: "The water was surrounded with huge nets, fastened between poles laid flat on the ground when ready for action, each net being perhaps sixty feet long and twenty feet deep. When all was ready, the pochards were frightened up out of the water. Like all diving ducks, they are obliged to fly low for some distance, and also to head the wind before rising. Just as the mass of birds reached the side of the pool, one of the immense nets, previously regulated by weights and springs, rose upright as it was freed from its fastenings by the fowler from a distance with a long rope. If this were done at the right moment, the ducks were met full in the face by a wall of net and thrown helpless into a deep ditch dug at its foot for their reception."

Most of the marine ducks are unfit for the table, the pochard and tufted ducks being exceptions—probably from the fact of their often resorting to fresh water. Akin to the last is the red-crested pochard or whistling duck—a rare British visitor, closely resembling its congener, but having a long silky crest on the head, and rich black neck, breast, and abdomen. The visits of this beautiful bird are very rare.

The scaup is another sea-duck which makes its appearance in autumn in large numbers, resorting to low oozy coasts, where it finds its food. This consists principally of shell-fish, especially mussels; hence it is sometimes called "musselduck." It is an expert diver, and a flock of hundreds of scaup may sometimes be seen to immerse themselves at the same moment. Like the division to which it belongs, the scaup is a heavy thick-set duck, and among the least eatable of its kind; yet hundreds are taken by the fishermen in their nets. Another of the winter ducks is the golden-eye, the mature male of which is among the handsomest and wariest of its kind. The golden-eye reaches our shores about the end of October; the great majority being birds of the year, with only a few matured males among them. Their extreme wariness makes it almost impossible to approach a flock, and when on sheets of fresh water they persistently keep near the middle. If the duck is difficult to come at by the shore-shooter or on land, it is equally puzzling to the puntsman. Instead of paddling away like other ducks when alarmed, it immediately takes wing, and after having dived, it can shoot from the water without waiting on the surface an instant. This species has also several remarkable characteristics. The members of a flock paddling in the sea are never all immersed at once, one or more always remaining on the surface as sentinels. Another trait is the almost invariable habit of nesting in holes, so that the Laps place darkened boxes by the sides of rivers and lakes for the ducks to lay in. Often as many as a dozen eggs are found, and the nests are lined with the soft down of the ducks. On our coasts these ducks feed upon crustaceans and molluscs, and many fishermen know it by the name of "mussel-cracker." "Rattlewing" is another provincial name owing to the musical whistle which the bird makes with its wings when flying. Its short rounded wings are ever restless; the shy little duck is ceaselessly swimming, diving, flying—never seeming to sleep and never still. The pride of plumage of the golden-eye stands it in little stead at table, where it is considered nearly worthless. An interesting incident which lingers in the writer's memory had for its subject a pair of male golden-eyes in all the glory of matured plumage A friend during a solitary ramble by a rush-grown mountain tarn had the good fortune to see these birds well within shot. Being a keen sportsman and fowler his fingers tingled to touch the trigger which should bring the rare prize to his hand. He was quite unaware of any other presence when a couple of shots awoke the echoes of the valley, and the ducks floated lifeless upon the water. When the white smoke lifted from the brush and reeds it showed the head and shoulders of a keen sporting friend of the first observer, and a beautiful drake now adorns the collection of each. The tufted duck is a prettily-marked species, and has the feathers on the back of the head elongated into a drooping crest. The upper plumage generally is black, flashing with green, bronze, and purple lustres, and the under plumage white. Although numbers of tufted ducks breed upon fresh water in this country, the great majority are only winter visitors, coming in October and leaving again in March. It rarely congregates in flocks, but is mostly found in scattered squadrons about shores and channels. Norfolk and Nottingham are the counties where the tufted ducks are known to breed, and here on decoys or in parks they find favourite retreats. The nest is made under a clump of grass or rushes, and from ten to thirteen eggs are laid.

Eider-ducks are among the most interesting of our sea-birds. Three species are found in this country; these are the common eider, the king eider, and Steller's eider.

The British eiders are essentially sea ducks— rarely even entering rivers, and seldom roving far inland. Occasionally found in our southern seas, they become more numerous as we ascend the east coast, until upon the Farnes, off Northumberland, we reach their most southern breeding haunts. On Holy Island and Lindisfarne a few pairs of St. Cuthbert's ducks have bred time out of mind. Except during times of nesting, the whole life of the bird seems spent upon the element whence it derives its food — crustaceans, namely—and this it always obtains by diving. In their northern breeding haunts the eiders begin to collect about the first week in May, and by the end of the third week most of the ducks have begun to lay. As soon as the colony has got well about this business the drakes leave the land, and for weeks may be seen between the islands, or spreading themselves down the coast-line in search of favourite feeding grounds. They never go far from the ducks however, nor do they at this time take long flights. In fact, the eider, unlike most ducks, is not migratory at any season, and seldom strays far from the spot where it was bred. During the nesting season, as at all others, the plumage of the male and female birds is very dissimilar. In the former, the upper part of the head is of a rich velvety black, while the sharply-contrasting neck and back are of the purest white; beneath, the plumage is black. At the same period the female is of a subdued rufous brown, with more or less dark markings; the tail feathers are now nearly black.

The colonies of breeding eiders often consist of an immense number of birds, and the nests lie so thickly together that it is difficult to avoid stepping into them. They are usually placed upon some slight elevation; and here in any faint depression the duck collects a small quantity of sea-weed and drift stuff, which she forms into a felty mass by kneading it with her breast. Upon this four or five eggs are laid in the course of a week; the eggs are pale green, rather like those of the heron. Even before the last egg is laid it is seen that a few feathers are scattered about the nest, and as incubation proceeds these increase in quantity. For the sitting bird covers her treasures over with down plucked from her breast; this she does day by day until a very considerable quantity buries the eggs. It is this down which has become such an important article of commerce. If the eiders are sitting under natural conditions the eggs are hatched in about twenty-six days, and the young birds are almost immediately taken down to the water. They show no hesitation in entering the sea,

P 2

and, once upon it, are quite at home. It is here that they sun themselves, feed, and sleep. On a rock-bound bit of coast it is interesting to watch the ducklings paddling along by the stones and feeding upon the tiny bivalves that are common along the bays and inlets.

These remarks refer to the breeding of wild eiders; but, unfortunately, colonies of birds under natural conditions are becoming more and more rare each year. The commercial collector has almost everywhere stepped in, and is putting a terrible drain upon this interesting species.

> "Where the brown duck strips her breast,
> For her dear eggs and windy nest,
> Three times her bitter spoil is won
> For woman; and when all is done
> She calls her snow-white piteous drake,
> Who plucks his bosom for our sake."

There is truth in these lines every one. In our own country the birds breed along the shores of the Firth of Forth, as well as in the Orkneys and Shetlands; on Colonsay and Islay it also abounds, and less frequently in many other northern breeding stations. It is in still more northern haunts, however, that the vast breeding colonies are found—in the Faroes, Iceland, and along the shores of the Scandinavian peninsula. In Norway, as in some other places, this bird is protected by law, though only to be persecuted the more persistently by private individuals. On one island, that of Isafjardarjup, the eider ducks are said to nest in thousands. Speaking of the breeding sites by the shore, Mr. Shepherd, who visited the colony, tells us that the brown ducks sat upon their nests in masses, and at every step started from beneath the feet. On this island, of three-quarters of a mile in length, it was difficult to walk without stepping into the nests. The island was one that was farmed. A thick stone breakwater ran along its coasts just above high-water mark. At the bottom and sides of the wall, alternate stones had been left out so as to form a series of compartments for the ducks to nest in. Every compartment was tenanted, and as the visitors walked along the ducks flew out all along the line. These were welcomed by the white drakes, which were tossing on the water, "with loud and clamorous cooing." A farmhouse on the island was tenanted in like manner. The house itself was "a great marvel." Ducks were hatching on the turf walls which surrounded it, in the window embrasures, on the ground, on the roof. "The house was fringed with ducks," and "a duck sat in the scraper." Then a grassy bank close by was cut into squares, every one of which was occupied. A windmill was packed; and so was every available object on the island—mounds, rock, and crevices. This was an eider-down farm. So tame were the ducks as to allow the farmer's wife to stroke them as they sat on their nests. Of course there is another side to this pleasant picture, as we see, when we learn how the "good lady" of the island repays the confidence of the birds. But we will allow Dr. Hartwig to tell it in his own way. He says :

"The eider-down is easily collected, as the birds are quite tame. The female having laid five or six pale greenish-olive eggs, in a nest thickly lined with her beautiful down, the collectors, after carefully removing the bird, rob the nest of its contents, after which they replace her. She then begins to lay afresh—though this time only three or four eggs — and again has recourse to the down of her body. But the greedy persecutors once more rifle her nest, and oblige her to line it for the third time. Now, however, her own stock of down is exhausted, and with a plaintive voice she calls her mate to her assistance, who willingly plucks the soft feathers from his breast to supply the deficiency. If the cruel robbery be again repeated, which in former times was frequently the case, the poor eider-duck abandons the spot, never to return, and seeks for a new home where she may indulge her maternal instinct undisturbed by the avarice of man."

Nature is prolific even in her waste ; but although eiders are plentiful, their breeding places are local, and this drain on them cannot long be continued without telling materially upon the species. In the locality referred to, each nest yields about one-sixth of a pound of down, worth from twelve to fifteen shillings a pound, and one pound and a half is required to make a single coverlet. The eggs are pickled for winter use, one or two only being left to hatch.

It need only be added that the eider is said to be the swiftest of all ducks, flying at the rate of nearly a hundred miles an hour.

Of the remaining rarer ducks are the ruddy-sheld, the long-tailed, and harlequin ducks. The ruddy-sheld is an exquisitely coloured duck with rufous plumage; and the harlequin, with its numerous bright colours, may be said to be the handsomest and rarest of all. The long tailed duck is sometimes called the sea-pheasant, and is not unfrequently found on our coasts in rough weather.

Duck decoying is one of the oldest methods of taking winter wild-fowl. It has been practised for centuries, and perhaps nowhere with greater success than in our own country. Owing to its insular position Britain has always been a great resort of fowl, and in times past it was visited by myriad of swans, geese, and ducks, many of which annually remained to breed. The marsh and fenlands of the south-eastern counties constituted tracts alike favourable for food and nesting, and for the most part the birds were undisturbed. But as the plough invaded their haunts the marsh was converted into corn-land, and from that time the breeding sea-fowl have steadily declined in numbers. The oldest decoys were merely adapted sheets of water, but when these, by virtue of having been drained, were no longer available, artificial ones were constructed in likely situations and planted round with timber to secure their privacy. Many of the decoys were farmed by fowlers, and the more valuable afforded a considerable source of revenue to the owners. Speaking of the dwellers in Croyland, Camden says that: "Their greatest gain is from the fish and wild ducks that they catch, which are so many, that in August they can drive at once into a single net three thousand ducks." He further adds that they call the pools in which the ducks are obtained their corn-fields, though there is no corn grown for miles round. For the privilege of taking fish and fowl three hundred pounds sterling were originally paid to the Abbots of Croyland, and afterwards to the king. Although the "driving of ducks" was allowed, a code of Fen laws decreed that neither nets nor engines should be used against the fowl "commonly called moulted ducks" before midsummer day yearly. In the early days of the decoys enormous quantities of fowl were taken in them. As many as 31,200 duck, teal, and widgeon were captured near Wainfleet in a single season, and 2,646 mallards in two days. In these early times it is said that a flock of wild ducks has been observed passing over the Fens in a continuous stream for eight hours together.

Lincolnshire is pre-eminently the land of wildfowl, and at one of the smallest decoys—that at Ashby—where the records have been carefully kept, it is seen that from 1833 to 1868, 48,664 ducks were captured in the pipes; 4,287 being the best take for any one year. Both now and in times past the ducks have always been sent to the London markets, and constitute an important food supply. The waters of the decoys are, of course, always fresh, and, being mostly frequented by the surface-feeding ducks, the great majority of the birds taken are held in estimation at table. It is true that widgeon and other of the diving ducks are sometimes driven to the decoys by rough sea weather, but these are too wary to enter the pipes, nor do they stay after the storms have abated. The ducks which constitute the commercial supply are mostly mallard and teal, with a few widgeon and a sprinkling of the rarer or marine forms according to season and the severity of the weather. I have before me a complete record of the fowl taken at one decoy for nearly a century, and this is interesting as showing not only the number of divers taken, but also a record of the species. That the migratory fowl return to the same waters year after year is confirmed by the fact that at the Ashby Decoy, already referred to, a "grey" duck with a conspicuous white neck spent eight winters there; and another abnormally coloured one visited it regularly for four or five years.

The duck decoys, once common throughout the country, fell into general disuse about the beginning of the present century; and their decline has been contemporaneous with the improvements made in firearms and all relating to shooting. Often as many marine ducks are bagged by one shot from a punt gun as the fowler can take in a day, and whilst the former can follow the birds, the latter must wait for their coming before he can commence decoying.

Duck decoying is one of the most interesting phases of woodcraft, and really skilled modern fowlers are as rare as trained falconers. Moreover, decoying is one of the fine arts. The decoy-man surrounds his craft with as much mystery as the old fish poacher his preparation of salmon roe, and fowling secrets are often kept in families for generations.

The best decoys are those about two or three acres in extent, and surrounded with wood. On larger ones fowl are difficult to work, and although there may be thousands on the water, none may be near enough to a "pipe" to regard either the dog or the "call" ducks. Before speaking of the actual working, it may be well to give a general outline of a decoy. Imagine then a stretch of water about the size indicated, and having five or six radiating arms or inlets— a figure represented exactly by a starfish, or the body and legs of a spider. The arms, called "pipes," curve away from the main pool so that it is impossible to see more than a short distance up them. They are also arranged that whichever way the wind blows, one or other of the pipes may be approached without getting to windward of the quick-scented fowl. The "pipes" are covered over with netting, and gradually diminish in height and width till they terminate in a "tunnel-net." Wooden palings bound these, built obliquely, over-lapping at regular intervals, and connected by low barriers. By this arrangement any one standing behind the palings is only visible to whatever is further up the "pipe," and cannot be seen by the occupants of the pool. This then is the general structure.

And now we must look to other matters essential to the general working of a decoy. About midsummer the "call" ducks are put upon the water, and their training is at once taken in hand. As this is an important part of the process, the ducks should be young, made very tame, and taught to come to any pipe from all parts of the pool when they are whistled. Previously these have been pinioned to prevent their flying away, and they cannot leave the lake. Still another requisite is a well-trained dog. Custom has always established that this shall be red and as "foxy"-looking as possible; and certainly dogs of this colour prove especially attractive to wildfowl.

About the beginning of September mallard and teal begin to congregate in the decoys, and a month later, if easterly winds prevail, there will probably be a flight of fowl from the north, consisting of mallards, teal, widgeon, pochards, and shovellers. These are attracted to the decoys by the resident birds, but more because it is their habit to fly off at dusk, and return at daybreak to sleep and enjoy themselves in the fancied security of the reedy pool.

Nothing requires more care and judgment than the successful decoying of ducks. It is carried on most successfully between nine and ten in the morning and three and four in the afternoon. In open weather the fowl are captured almost entirely by means of the dog, but as soon as frost sets in they are taken by feeding them in the pipe, and keeping a piece of water constantly open near it. Now as to the actual working. If the birds are sluggish the trained dog cleverly works them from the bank, and either drives or attracts them by curiosity to the pipe to be worked, being also aided by the decoy ducks and induced to stay by finding corn scattered about. By skilful manipulation the fowl are worked up the pipe, the dog trotting in and out of the reed-screens and luring them further and further away. Soon they have made sufficient progress to enable the man to show himself, and this he does at the same time waving his hat. Retreat to the pool is cut off, and the terrified birds rush up the pipe only to find themselves in the narrowing tunnel-net which terminates it. This is at once detached, and the final scene is the wringing of the ducks' necks by the decoy man. As all the pipes curve to the right the decoying is unseen from the pool, and one set of fowl can be "worked" whilst others are sleeping or preening themselves on the lake. Further aids of concealment for the working of the decoy other than those enumerated are banks of earth and brushwood running parallel to the palings.

As sportsmen would rather shoot fowl than snare them, the decoy is mostly interesting nowadays to naturalists and antiquarians. To show their value, however, in times gone by, it may be mentioned that a corporation has been known to invest trust funds in one, and that a decoy in Suffolk, which sent a ton and a half of wild-fowl to London four times a week, realised £1,000 a year. In this 16,800 ducks were captured in a single season.

CHAPTER XI.

FIELD AND COVERT POACHERS.

As compared with the doings of human "mouchers," there is a class of field poachers whose depredations are tenfold more destructive. These are nature's poachers, and their vigils never cease. In season and out, by night and by day, they harry the things of the field and wood. Playing as some say a questionable part in the economy of nature, they play a very certain part in the economy of our game, both winged and furred. Strange anomaly it is, that whilst our game stock could not be preserved a year without their agency, the hand of every one is against them. So long as nature is founded on its present beneficent plan, so long will the swallow be speared by the shrike, and every wood be the scene of plunder and prey. Nature is one with rapine, and the close observance of every woodland way only emphasises the fact. Every sylvan thing is but a unit in a possible chain of destruction. The bee-bird captures the butterfly, and is stricken down in the act by the hawk; the keeper kills the raptor, and the keeper's hobnobbing with death is delayed but a while.

The greatest and smallest murder but to live, and whilst the eagle kills the lordly stag, the merlin is lark-hawking on the down. Only those whose harvest is gleaned in the open, who have observed in all weathers and through every hour of the day and night, can form any adequate conception of how dependent is one form of life upon another. The way of an eagle in the air is one of those things concerning which Solomon professed himself unable to understand, and the scythe-like sweep of wings of the majestic bird is one of the most glorious sights which nature has to offer. Just as the eagle is the largest, so the merlin is the smallest British bird of prey, and to see this miniature falcon rush past on the breast of a mountain storm gives an idea of its almost marvellous velocity of flight. Within the whole range of animate nature, nowhere is the adaptation of means to an end more strikingly exhibited than among the raptors—the plunderers. The furred poachers are not less appropriately fitted with their weapons of destruction; and so perfectly adapted is the otter to its environment that its movements in the water are as the very poetry of motion.

Let us follow these poachers of the field and covert to their haunts, and there observe them in their wild home. The sparrow-hawk is a roving arab of the air and the most arrant of poachers. Ask the keeper to detail to you the character of this daring marauder, and he will record a black and bloody list of depredations against the bird. He knows nothing, however, of the laws which govern the economy of nature, and if he did, or would, what are they compared to the shilling per head for those he can display on the vermin-rails.

The kestrel or windhover acts in quite a different fashion to the sparrow-hawk. It is persecuted less, and confidently approaches human habitations. And yet at certain seasons the kestrel is as destructive in the covert as its congeners. When the pheasants represent little more than balls of down he clutches them from out the grass as he clutches a mouse or cockchafer. Coming from out the blue, one hears the pleasant cry of kee, kee, keelie, and there he hangs rapidly vibrating his wings, yet as stationary as though suspended by a silken thread. Presently down he comes, plump as a stone, and without touching the ground sweeps a "cheeper" from off it, and soars high above the covert. The depredations are only committed, however, when the game is exceedingly small, and the benefit which the kestrel confers on the woods by its presence far outweighs any harm it may do. The artificial methods of game-rearing now in vogue are most conducive to disease. In extenuation of the thefts of our little marauders it may be pleaded that they invariably pick off the weak and ailing birds, and therefore tend to the survival of robust and healthy stock.

The presiding spirits of the moors are the beautiful little merlins. They work together, and quarter the heather like a brace of well-broken pointers. Not an object escapes them. However closely it may conform to its environment, or however motionless remain, it is detected by the sharp eye of the merlin and put away. The miniature falconry in which the merlin indulges on the open moorlands, where nothing obstructs the view, is one of the most fascinating sights in nature. The "red hawk" is plucky beyond its size and strength, and will pull down a partridge, as we have witnessed repeatedly. The young of moorfowl, larks, pipits, and summer snipe constitute its food on the fells. It lays four bright red eggs in a depression among the heather, and about this are strewn the remains of the birds indicated. To be seen to advantage this smallest of British falcons ought to be seen in its haunts. It is little larger than a thrush, and in the days of falconry was flown by ladies, its game being larks, pipits, pigeons, and occasionally partridges. On the moorlands it may be seen suddenly to shoot from a stone, encircle a tract of heather, and then return to its perch. A lark passes over its head, and its wings are raised and its neck outstretched; but it closes them as if unwilling to pursue the bird. Then it flies, skimming low over the furze and heather, and alights on a granite boulder similar to the one it has just left. As we approach, the male and female flap unconcernedly off, and beneath the block are remains of golden plover, ling birds, larks, and young grouse.

At night the waterside is productive of life, and here it is most varied. Like most poachers, the heron is a night fisher, and there is one equally destructive which carries on its nefarious trade under the full light of day—the kingfisher. And the kingfisher is a poacher in another respect. It never constructs the hole in which its young is reared, but takes possession of that of some small burrowing rodent, or even that of the little sand-martin.

The buzzard is another bird of the moorlands, but can hardly be convicted of poaching. When it takes moor-game these are invariably found to be diseased or late hatched birds, and it certainly has not speed to pull down a full-grown grouse. Many times during whole summer afternoons have we seen the buzzards wheeling about when the young grouse have been following the brooding birds, but never have we seen them swoop at one. And seeing that as many as sixty mice have been taken from the crop of a single bird, surely the buzzard ought to be protected. During times of severe frost the buzzard often performs deeds of daring to obtain a meal. When a lad, Wordsworth was in the habit of setting "gins" for woodcocks, and one morning on going to examine his snares he discovered a buzzard near one which was struck. The bird of prey attempted to escape, but being held fast could not. A woodcock had been taken in one of the snares, which when fluttering had been seen and attacked by the buzzard. Not content, however, with the body of the woodcock, it had swallowed a leg also, round which the nooze was drawn, and the limb was so securely lodged in the latter's stomach that no force that the bird could exert could withdraw it.

In the glades and woodlands the garrulous blue-jay is a sad pilferer, to say nothing of its poaching propensities. In the spring it sucks innumerable eggs, and makes free right and warren of the peas and beans in the keeper's garden, and those sown in the glades for the pheasants; and so the old man's whole knowledge of woodcraft is directed against it. In addition to this, the jay does indirect harm, which multiplies the cunning engines devised for its destruction. For by pilfering the crops before mentioned, which are planted with the object of keeping the wandering pheasants on the land, a poor show of birds may be the result when October comes round, and the keeper's reputation suffers. Even the audacious pies steal both pheasant and partridge chicks, and consequently each find a place in the "larder." The brown-owl is mostly a rabbit poacher, but its congener, the barn-owl, poaches to good effect, as a subsequent statement will show. Almost all the birds of the crow-kind are persistent poachers, and are generally shot down.

It is probable that the number of grouse on the higher hill ranges is very much kept in check by the great number of carrion-crows which everywhere exist among the fells. They impale the eggs of the red grouse upon their bills, and carry them away to eat at leisure. Under some wall or rock great numbers of egg-shells may often be found, testifying to the havoc which these sable marauders commit. This bird is one of the great features of the northern fell fauna, and is well known to the dalesmen and shepherds, who give it a bad character. In spite of much persecution, however, it is still a common resident, keeping to the sheep-walks in search of food, and breeding among the mountains. Although a great carrion-feeder, it will kill weak and ailing lambs, picking out the eyes and tongues of these when they are reduced to a helpless condition. They are resident birds in the north, and only the snows of winter drive them to the lowlands in search of food. As the hooded crow is only a seasonable visitor, it is but little felt as a poacher. The keeper has the shrikes or butcher-birds in his black list, but these do little harm, as their shambles in the blackthorns abundantly prove.

Mention of the noble peregrine marks a poacher of the first water. As the bird sits watching from the jag of a mountain crag, it is the very emblem of passive speed and strength. Nowhere but in the birds' haunts can these attributes be seen to perfection. A trained falcon is slow of flight and uncertain of aim as compared with a wild bird. Its symmetry, its stretch of wing, its keen eyes and cruel talons, all speak to the same end. While some of the larger hawks are treated with indifference by the bird-world, not so the peregrine. A pair of buzzards pass over, but the cheep and chatter of field and hedgerow go on. A peregrine sails down dale and all is hushed! A strange experience this at noon in the heyday of summer —but the shadow of the peregrine stills all life. A terrified screech is heard, and bird life seeks the thickest retreats. The depredations of the peregrine are greatest, of course, during the breeding season; and at this time it even carries off the newly-born lambs of the small, black-faced mountain sheep. Now hardly anything comes amiss. Partridges, ducks, pheasants, hares, grouse, plover—each is taken in turn, and the birds forage over a wide area. A barndoor fowl sometimes supplies a meal, or a dead sheep (so long as the flesh is sweet), thrushes, pigeons, gulls, and a number of water and shore-haunting birds. Once scrambling among boulders in search of Alpine plants, a large bird of prey was seen advancing on the wing. At a distance the under-parts appeared white, but the bird, coming directly over, enabled us to recognise distinctly the dark bars across the feathers of the abdomen. Its flight under these circumstances was a sort of flapping motion, not unlike that of a ringdove; and its head turned rapidly in various directions, the eye peering into the rocks and crannies of the ghylls in search of any skulking prey. Soon this silent hunting was all changed. Above us was a ledge covered with blood, bones, and feathers. We were close to the nest. Just as we were discovered one of the falcons went "whizz" past our face, almost touching it. Then it gives a wild yelp, as in one gyration it shoots upwards, and screams round the crag. Again the bird dashes along the cliff, and is joined by the female, who from her nest has been quietly watching us. The peregrine's outstretched wings measure three feet, and it makes a velocity of fifty-seven miles an hour. One at the above rate flew one thousand three hundred and fifty miles. So great is its power and speed of flight that a bird belonging to Colonel Thornton was seen to cut a snipe in two in mid-air.

Falcons will occasionally search after their prey when it has been driven to seek shelter from the closeness of pursuit. The goshawk, which falconers use mostly for taking hares and rabbits, frequently does this, and will watch for hours when its game has taken to cover. As well as ground-game the goshawk poaches pheasants and partridges, numbers of these being killed by the bird in its wild state. Through a wooded country it pursues its quarry with great dexterity; and it possesses great powers of abstinence. During the day it remains solitary in dark fir-woods, coming out to feed at morning and evening. . . . .

We advance over the heather; and there, skimming towards us, is a large hawk—a harrier. As it flies near the ground, working as a pointer or setter would do, the species cannot be doubted. Now it stoops, glides, ascends, stoops again, and shoots off at right angles. Rounding a shoulder of a hill, it drops in a dark patch of ling. A covey of young grouse whirr heavily over the nearest brae—but the marsh harrier remains. It has struck down a "cheeper," and is dragging its victim to the shelter of a furze-bush. A male and female harrier invariably hunt in consort, and afford a pleasant sight as they "harry" the game, driving it from one to the other, and hawking in the most systematic fashion. They thoroughly work the ground previously marked out, generally with success. In hawking the quiet mountain tarns their method is regulated according to circumstance. In such case they not unfrequently sit and watch, capturing their prey by suddenly pouncing upon it.

At one time the golden and white-tailed eagles bred not uncommonly in the mountainous environment of the English Lake District. Most majestic of the winged poachers, they held sway over a wide area, and suffered no intrusion. The eyries were perched high upon the almost inaccessible fastnesses of the mountains. It is asserted by the shepherds of the district that the eagles during the breeding season destroyed a lamb per day, to say nothing of the carnage made on hares, partridge, pheasants, grouse, and the water-fowl that inhabit the lakes. The farmers and dalesmen were always careful to plunder the eyries, but not without considerable risk to life and limb. A man was lowered from the summit of the precipitous rocks by a rope of fifty fathoms, and was compelled to defend himself from attack during his descent. The poet Gray in his *Journal* graphically describes how the eyries were annually plundered, upon one of which occasions he was present. Wordsworth says that the eagles built in the precipices overlooking one of the tarns in the recesses of Helvellyn, and that the bird used to wheel and hover over his head as he fished in the silent tarn. Now the spot is occupied by a pair of patriarchal ravens—the sole remaining relics of the original "Red Tarn Club."

Among the mountains an instance is related of an eagle which having pounced on a shepherd's dog, carried it to a considerable height; but the weight and action of the animal effected a partial liberation, and he left part of his flesh in the eagle's beak. The dog was not killed by the fall; he recovered of his wound, but was so intimidated that he would never go that way again. Subsequently the owner of the dog shot at and wounded one of the eagles. The bird, nearly exhausted, was found a week afterwards by a shepherd of Seatoller; its lower mandible was split, and the tongue wedged between the interstices. The bird was captured and kept in confinement, but it became so violent that ultimately it had to be destroyed. On the eagles being frequently robbed of their young in Greenup they removed to the opposite side of the crag. At this place they built for two years, but left it for Raven Crag, within the Coom, where, after staying one year only, they returned to their ancient seat in Eagle Crag; here they built annually during their stay in Borrowdale. On the loss of its mate the remaining eagle left the district, but returned the following spring with another. This pair built during fourteen years in Borrowdale, but finally abandoned it for Eskdale. At the last-mentioned place they were also disturbed, and the female eagle being afterwards shot the male flew off and returned no more.

The white-tailed sea eagles bred upon the rocks of a towering limestone escarpment overlooking a recess of the sea, and fed upon gulls and terns. The vast peat mosses which stretched away for miles below them abounded with hares and grouse, and among these the birds made devastation. Year after year they carried off their young from the same cliffs, and now return only at rare intervals when storm driven. The peregrines have the eagles' eyrie, and are only eagles in miniature. The sea-fowl form their food in summer, as do wild ducks in winter. At this latter season the osprey or "fish-hawk" comes to the bay and the still mountain tarns, adding wildness to the scenes which his congeners have left never to return.

Those who have recently advocated a close time for owls have, fortunately, been forestalled by legislation. The Act of 1881 affords protection to all wild birds during the breeding season, and, although exemption is allowed in favour of owners and occupiers of land, owls, being included in the schedule, may not be destroyed even by them or with their authority. It was a wise step that granted this double protection, for of all birds, from the farmers' standpoint, owls are the most useful. These birds hunt silently and in the night, and are nothing short of lynx-eyed cats with wings. The benefit they confer upon agriculturists is most incalculable, which is susceptible of proof.

It is well known that owls hunt by night, but it may be less a matter of common knowledge that, like other birds of prey, they return by the mouth the hard indigestible parts of their food in the form of elongated pellets. These are found in considerable quantities about the birds' haunts, and an examination of them reveals the fact that owls prey upon a number of predacious creatures the destruction of which is directly beneficial to man. Of course, the evidence gained in this way is infallible, and to show to what extent owls assist in preserving the balance of nature, it may be mentioned that seven hundred pellets examined yielded the remains of sixteen bats, three rats, two hundred and thirty-seven mice, six hundred and ninety-three voles, one thousand five hundred and ninety shrews, and twenty-two birds. These truly remarkable results were obtained from the common barn-owl, and the remains of the twenty-two birds consisted of nineteen sparrows, one greenfinch, and two swifts. The tawny and long-eared owls of our woodlands are also mighty hunters, and an examination of their pellets showed equally interesting results. It must be remembered in this connection that Britain is essentially an agricultural country, and that if its fauna is a diminutive one it is not less formidable. We have ten tiny field creatures constituting an army in themselves, which if not kept under would quickly devastate our fields. These ten species consist of four mice, three voles, and three shrews. Individually, so tiny are these that any one species could comfortably curl itself up in the divided shell of the horse-chestnut. But farmers well know that if these things are small they are no means to be despised. Now that the corn crops are cut and the hay housed, the field vole and meadow mouse are deprived of their summer shelter. Of this the barn-owl is perfectly aware, and at evening he may be seen sweeping low over the meadows seeking whom he may devour. And with what results we already know.

Much unnatural history has been written of the owls, and unfortunately most people have their ideas from the poets.

The barn-owl, when she has young, brings to her nest a mouse every twelve minutes, and, as she is actively employed both at evening and dawn, and both male and female hunt, forty mice a day is the lowest computation we can make. How soft is the plumage of the owl, and how noiseless her flight! Watch her as she floats past the ivy tod, down by the ricks, and silently over the old wood. Then away over the meadows, through the open door and out of the loop-hole in the barn, round the lichened tower, along the course of the brook. Presently she returns to her four downy young, with a mouse in one claw and a vole in the other, soon to be ripped up, torn, and eaten by the greedy snapping imps. The young are produced from April to December, and not unfrequently both young and eggs are found in the same nest. If you would see the mid-day *siesta* of the owls, climb up into some hay-mow. There in an angle of the beam you will see their owlships, snoring and blinking wide their great round eyes. Their duet is the most unearthly, ridiculous, grave, like-nothing-else noise you ever heard. Here they will stay all day, digesting the mice with which they have largely gorged themselves, until twilight, when they again issue forth on their madcap revellings. This clever mouser, then, this winged cat, has a strong claim to our protection. So let not idle superstition further its destruction.

The keeper's indiscretions are fewer in fur than in feather. His larder abounds in long-bodied creatures of the weasel kind. Here is the richly-coloured dark-brown fur of the pine-martin; that of the polecat, loose and light at the base but almost black at the extremity; and there are many skins of weasels, reddish brown above with the sides and under parts white. For each of these creatures he has quaint provincial names of his own. The pine-martin he calls the "sweet-mart," in contradistinction to the polecat, which is the "foumart," or "foulmart"— a name bestowed on the creature because it emits a secretion which has an abominable stench. Also, we have the stoat or ermine, which even with us is white in winter, brown in summer; but the tip of the tail is always black.

The beautiful martins take up their abode in the rockiest parts of the wood where the pines grows thickly. They are strictly arboreal in their habits; and, seen among the shaggy pine foliage, the rich yellow of their throats is sharply set off by the deep brown of the thick glossy fur. With us they do not make their nests and produce their young in the pine-trees, but among the loose craggy rocks. Martins rarely show themselves till evening. They prey upon rabbits, hares, partridges, pheasants, and small birds; and when we say that, like the rest of the mustelidæ, they kill for the love of killing, it is not hard to understand why the keeper's hand is against them. Sometimes they do great harm in the coverts; and the old man shoots them, traps them, and does them to death with various subtle engines of his own machination. To-day the martin is rare; soon it will be extinct altogether. Weasels do much less harm. They are the smallest of our carnivorous animals, and will probably long survive. They frequently abound where least suspected, in the cultivated as well as the wildest parts of the district. They take up their abode near farmhouses, in decayed outbuildings, hay-ricks, and disused quarries; and may often be seen near old walls or running along the top of them with a mouse or bird in their mouths. These things form the staple of their food; but there is no denying that a weasel will occasionally run down the strongest hare, and that rabbits, from their habit of rushing into their burrows become an easy prey. But this does not happen often, I believe. To rats the weasel is a deadly enemy; no united number of them will attack it, and the largest singly has no chance against it. Like the polecat the weasel hunts by scent. It climbs trees easily and takes birds by stealth. The keeper has seen a brooding partridge taken in this manner, and on winter evenings the sparrows roosting in holes in a hay-rick. Weasels also kill toads and frogs; and their mode of killing these, as well as of despatching birds, is by piercing the skull.

The polecat, or fitchet, keeps much to the woods, and feeds mostly on rabbits and game.

But in the northern fell districts it often takes up a temporary abode on the moors during the season that grouse are hatching. Then it not only kills the sitting birds but sucks the eggs, and thus whole broods are destroyed. Many "cheepers" of course fall victims. Knowing well the ferocity of the polecat, I believe the damage done to grouse moors where this bloodthirsty creature takes up its abode can hardly be estimated. Like others of its tribe, the polecat kills more prey than it needs. Sometimes it makes an epicurean repast from the brain alone. Fowl-houses suffer considerably from its visits; and it has been known to kill and afterwards leave untouched as many as sixteen large turkeys. In the nest of a fitchet which was observed to frequent the banks of a stream no fewer than eleven fine trout were found. The gamekeeper persistently dogs this creature both summer and winter. In the latter season every time it ventures abroad it registers its progress through the snow. It is then that the old man is most active in his destruction, and most successful. He tracks the vermin to some stone fence or disused quarry or barn, cuts off the enemy's retreat, and then unearths him. Trapped he is at all times.

The stoat or ermine is as destructive to covert game as the animals just mentioned. Upon occasion it destroys great quantities of rats, and this is its only redeeming quality. Partridge, grouse, and pheasants all fall a prey to the stoat, and hares when pursued by it seem to become thoroughly demoralised. Water is no obstacle to the ermine, and it climbs trees in search of squirrels, birds, and eggs. A pair of stoats took up their abode in a well-stocked rabbit warren. The legitimate inmates were killed off by wholesale, and many were taken from the burrows with the skull empty. The stoat progresses by a series of short quick leaps, which enable it to cover the ground more quickly than could possibly be imagined for so small an animal.

Enough has been said to sketch the characters of these creatures, and to justify their presence in the larder. Interesting in themselves as wild denizens of the woods, they would be fatal to game-preserving.

Vulpecide is no great crime in the north. Foxes abound in the fastnesses of the fells, and the little wiry foxhounds that hunt the mountains in winter account for but few in a season; and so it devolves upon the shepherds and gamekeepers and farmers to deal with them. This they do irrespective of season; if allowed to live, the foxes would destroy abundance of lambs in spring. They are tracked through the snow in winter, shot in summer, and destroyed wholesale when they bring their young to the moors in autumn. It therefore happens that even the bright red fur of the fox may be seen on the keeper's gibbet.

Hedgehogs are taken in steel traps baited with a pheasant's or a hen's egg. At times squirrels are killed in hundreds, but they do not grace the larder, neither do the spiny hedgehogs. Squirrels bark young trees, especially ash-stoles and holly.

Occasionally a creature more rare than the rest adorns the larder. The old keepers remember a white-tailed eagle and a great snowy owl. Sometimes a peregrine is shot, and more rarely, in autumn, a hobby or a goshawk. A miscellaneous row on the vermin rails comprises moles, weasels, and cats. The mole is libelled by being placed there; he is a destroyer of many creatures which are injurious to land. Domestic cats soon revert to a semi-wild state when once they take to the woods, and are terribly destructive in the coverts. They destroy pheasants, partridges, leverets, and rabbits. The life of these wild tabbies is wild indeed. Every dormant instinct is aroused; each movement becomes characteristically feline; and when these creatures revert to life in the woods it is impossible to reclaim them. Climatic influences work remarkable changes upon the fur, causing it to grow longer and thicker; and the cats take up their abode in stony crevasse or hollow tree. In summer, when kittens are produced, the destruction of game is almost incredible.

Under the dark slab by the river the otters breed; but it is impossible to dislodge them. Iron-sinewed shaggy otterhounds have tried, but never with success. The fishermen complain of the quantity of fish which the otter destroys. Trout are found dead on the rocks; salmon are there bitten in the shoulder but only partially eaten.

CHAPTER XII.

HOMELY TRAGEDY.

I.

IN our summer fishings, one of the spots to which we used to resort was a quaint cottage in the vale of Duddon—the Duddon that Wordsworth has immortalised in his series of sonnets. The cottage stood hard by the stream, and in it lived a widow woman, the daughter of a hill "statesman." During trout-time the house was embowered in greenery. Deliciously cool was its whitewashed porch and clean sanded floor, a great tree standing over all. In the grate of her parlour in summer, where Mr. Wordsworth often used to sit, she invariably had a thick sod of purple heather in full bloom. To the stream many anglers came, and drew from their holds the pink-spotted trout. The dipper and kingfisher darted by the door, and those who drank in the quiet and pastoral peace of Duddon never forgot it. The woman of the cottage, by great industry and exertion, had reared and settled comfortably in life a large family. She was respected by all about her. Out of her small means she gave away almost as much food and home-brewed ale as was sold by any inn of the country-side. For one in so limited a sphere in life hers was almost an ideal one ; and yet her end was terribly tragic. She left home one wintry afternoon to visit a sick relation in Eskdale. At this time " pedlars"—of whom the Wanderer of " *The Excursion* " is a type—were common in remote country districts ; and one of these offered to convey her in his gig to her destination over the Birk-Moor road. At the end of this he was to take her up at a stated time. It happened that she was too late for the traveller, but walked onward, supposing that he was behind and would overtake her. On the sixth day after this, the clergyman's daughter from Eskdale casually called at the poor woman's cottage. It then became known that she had not been seen at Eskdale, and a band of dalesfolk at once set out to search the Fells. The body of the poor creature was found only forty yards from the road, her hands and knees terribly lacerated and her dress torn. These showed that after losing the power of walking she had struggled on, no one knows how far, upon her hands and knees. She had taken out her spectacles, as was thought, to assist her in seeing her way through the blinding mists. These had prevailed for a week, and to them must be attributed the fact that her body lay so long undiscovered on the mountain road. Some sweetmeats tied in a handkerchief, which she had carried for her grandchildren, were found near the spot where she died.

None but those who have been caught in them can form any idea of how terrible are mountain snowstorms. Blinding and bewildering, both men and animals quickly succumb to them. Clouds and banks of snow rush hither and thither in opaque masses ; the bitter hail and sleet seem to drive through you. A few moments after the storm breaks every wrap is soaked through ; the cold is intense, and a sense of numbness soon takes possession of the entire body. Twice has the writer narrowly escaped death on the northern mountains in winter, deliverance upon one occasion being made barely in time by a search-party of shepherds.

Easdale is one of the most picturesque glens among the Cumbrian mountains—"a spot made by nature for herself." With its tarn, its ghyll-contained waterfall, and the fact of its being placed among the splintery peaks of the Borrowdale series, it constitutes a wildly charming spot at every season. Here upon the snow, many years ago, was played a cruel tragedy indeed. A poor hard-working peasant and his wife, named Green, were returning from Langdale late on a wintry evening to their home in Easdale. A terrible storm overtook them on the way, and, becoming exhausted, both died in it. Meanwhile six children were snow-bound in their cottage, where, without help, they remained several days. Fully appreciating their situation, but as yet ignorant of the fate which had befallen their parents, a little lass of nine assumed command and exhibited unusual forethought and care in meeting the home wants of her brothers and sisters. After some days she made her escape from the cottage, and told the hill shepherds how her father and mother had failed to return. A search party was organised; and after some time the bodies were discovered upon the hills at a short distance from each other.

II.

The wheatears love to haunt the old wall, and in summer are never far from it. In one of its niches they have their pale blue eggs. The wall runs by the side of the fells. The grass on its side is green as the water runs down them from the crags. The wall has a fauna and a flora all its own. In the interstices of the stones spleenwort and the parsley-fern grow; there are mosses and lichens too, and stone-crop. A few grasses wave airily on the scant mound at the top. A foxglove with its purple fingers grows solitary. Two species of shelled snail take harbour in the wall—one of them the beautiful *Helix nemoralis*. There are insects innumerable, bronze and gilded flies, and spiders that hang out their golden webs to the dews of morning. These are festooned from stone to stone, and are productions of the night. Weasels love the old wall, mice hide beneath it, and from it in spring the hedgehog rolls, its spines covered with dead oak leaves. Sometimes the fox, as it leaves its green "benk" in the crags, runs along its summit. Harebells nod at its foot, as do green-smelling brackens. Mountain blackbirds perch upon it, and stonechats and pipits.

Half-way down the wall, on its near side, is a sad green spot. Beside it we have thrown up a loose, lone cairn. It happened in winter when the fells were white. The snows had fallen thickly for many days; all the deep holes were filled up, and the mountain road was no longer to be seen. The wall tops stood as white ridges on the otherwise smooth surface. Only the crags hung in shaggy, snowy masses, black seams and scars picking out the dread ravines. Nature was sombre and still. It seemed as though her pulse had ceased to beat. The softly winnowed snowflakes still fell, and not even the wing of a bird of prey wafted the cold, thin air. It had gone hard with the sheep. Hundreds were buried in the snow, and would have to be dug out. They sought the site of the old wall, and fell into the deepest drifts. Only the hardy goatlike herdwicks instinctively climbed to the bleak and exposed fell tops. In this was their safety. To relieve the sheep that had as yet escaped, hay was carried to the Fells. Each shepherd had a loose bundle upon his back. It was thus, with the three dogs, that we toiled up the gorge, by an undefined route, parallel to the buried fence. Soon it commenced to snow heavily, and the sky suddenly darkened. The dogs that were in front stopped before some object. They whined, ran towards us, and gave out short, sharp barks. With a kind of instinctive dread we followed them. They led us on to a granite boulder; on its lee side lay something starkly outlined against the snow. *Dead!* we whispered to each other. There was no trace of pain—nothing but quiet peace. The icy fingers grasped a pencil, and on the snow lay a scrap of paper. It contained only two words— " *This day* "—nothing more.

It was Christmas. In silent benediction the snow-flakes fell upon him, and as these formed a pure white shroud, his face seemed touched with the light of ineffable love. We buried him next day in the little mountain cemetery. Whence he came, or whither he went, none ever knew. A few belongings—paltry enough—are thrust in a hole in the old barn for *her*. How precious, too, God knows, if ever she should come that way.

This cold, still, dead thing, is a sad association, —but it will remain.

III.

A green mountain slope, with red outcroppings here and there, had originally suggested untold treasure in the shape of rich iron ore. This had produced, as the hill-side abundantly showed, the various stages of mining enthusiasm. But the ordinary processes of nature would, in this case, seem to have been reversed; and so it came about that the wildest dreams of the prospectors were never to be realised. The rich red rock which showed at the top degenerated in quality in exact ratio as it gained in depth. And this fact it was that cost the original holders so many thousands of pounds. Never had speculation seemed less speculative. But, instead of being buried in the inmost recesses of the mountain, the absolutely pure ironstone cropped up among the brackens, picking out their tender green with its deep earthy stains. Nuggets knocked from the "leads" were dense and heavy to the hand, and mutely asked but to be worked to be transmuted into gold. It needed but little persuasion for men to embark in this undertaking, and that little was furnished by the mining engineers. Their reports were as glowing as the red ironstone itself. Then active operations were commenced. Every one concerned threw himself vigorously into the work, and a valley previously unknown became as active as an invaded anthill. Stalwart miners came there with "kit" and tools, men skilled in their work, who had disembowelled the mountains of Cumberland and Cornwall. These men occupied the wooden "shanties" that had been hastily erected for them; and, as they took the sun among the birch and hazel bushes on Sundays, dreamt over the dreams of the sanguine proprietors.

It were well, however, to draw a veil over all subsequent proceedings. Nature, for her part, has already done so. The torn and abraded hill-sides have lost their harsh outlines, and a veil of kindly mantling green has spread itself over all. True, as in other similar enterprises, there are still traces of the useless essay—the dull prosaic record of half-finished ditches, purposeless shafts, untenable pits, abandoned engines, and meaningless disruptions of the soil upon the mountain—and a railway.

This last was one of the details of the original enterprise, and cost £100,000. It is still in operation, runs for no one in particular, and but for few folk in general. Its way lies along a beautiful valley hemmed in by the mountains where the line ends. There is no way out of the vale except by walking over the hills, and only a few straggling tourists ever invade it. We take the train at its junction with an insignificant loop-line, and accompany it to its destination. We are booked by an all-important official, who is a compound of many individuals. He issues tickets, is guard, porter, station master, and signalman in one. These offices apply not to one station alone, but to four. In addition he is general superintendent, and directs the lad who drives the engine. We have said that the route of the line is up a narrow gorge-like valley; and this has a decided incline over the dozen miles of its sinuous course. Here everything is primitive, and there is no great necessity to conform to coventional rules. The carriages, even the "first-class" ones, are hardly constructed with a view to comfort; and, when you get tired of the jolting of these, the factotum alluded to has no objection to stopping the train so that you may get out and walk. Even if you stop to gather wild flowers—and the valley here is a wild-flower paradise—you may soon, by a sharp trot, catch the train again, even if it be going at its lightning express speed, so to speak. Daily the goatlike herdwicks stray on to the line from the neighbouring knolls; and occasionally you are asked to throw stones at the little mountain sheep, so that the train may speed on its way. Mr. General Superintendent will give you permission to shoot rabbits from the moving train. It was while thus engaged that the whole thing came to a sudden stop. Upon looking out to learn why, we saw a couple of dalesfolk walking leisurely towards us, and wanting to know, "What o'clock it might be—by the day." At another point along the line we stopped to replenish the engine with water. This was done from a disused grocery box, into which the tricklings from the hill-side were directed by a bit of wood hollowed in the form of a spout. The engine-boy sat upon the box, whistling through the process, which occupied an unconscionable time. He was a lad with a pleasant face, who amused himself when the train was in progress by pelting the birds and sheep with bits of coal from the tender.

Before long, I take it, all trace of the White Quartz Valley Railway will have vanished. Its plant is decaying, and soon will fall away. Swallows have built beneath the rafters of the miners' sheds, at evening bats fly in and out at the open doors, and a pair of screech-owls that have taken up their abode declare the place as desolate. There is only one person in the country-side who has yet any lingering faith in the railway, the mine, or the mountain. This is an old miner, himself like a nugget of iron ore. He has infinite faith in a deep compensating future, and bides his time. When mellowed by ale and the soothing fumes of a short black pipe, he assures you that he will stand by the mountain through fair weather or foul. And if you evince any interest in his oft-told tale and have gained his confidence, he will take down an old gunpowder canister and reveal to you the substance of his faith.

"Them there shares, as was give to me by Lord L—— hissel', is worth a matter o' £2,000 o' solid gold if ever them mines should yield. That's the valley on 'em, as is writ in black and white inside. Two hundred shares at £10 apiece is £2,000. I've reckoned it times and again. Me lord gev' em to me wi' 'is own 'ands, and he says, says he, 'Mould' some day, maybe, ye'll become a rich man."

But Mould never did become rich; and this is how it came about.

For months we had been under the unbroken dominion of ice and snow. Many of those who had attained to a garrulous old age lamented the cessation of what they called "old-fashioned" winters for the last time. The snow fell thickly, and as it came through a thin, biting air it was frozen ere it reached the ground. Neither man nor beast nor bird could break through the hard, glistening crust. As many of the stone fences as were not completely buried, were scalloped and fluted in most fantastic fashion. Everywhere was one wide, white expanse; and a silence that might be felt covered the land. The hill districts were terrible in their loneliness; and every frost seemed to deepen the desolation. But at the end of six silent weeks there came a great change. A soft, warm wind set in from the south, bringing heavy rain-clouds. First the snow of the lower lands became honeycombed, then was dissolved by the night rains. Black seams and scars picked out the dread ravines of the hills; and the fell becks tore down the slopes bearing tons of loose *débris*. The valleys became river-beds, and masses of brown water rushed off to the sea. In thirty-six hours the transformation was complete, and striking beyond description. The burst of life and the babel of sounds were almost bewildering. The air was filled with the flutter of wings and voices of birds. In short, by sea or by land, never was there a more sudden change. A new element was in the air, and the older farmers averred that there had been a "ground thaw"—an event as rare, according to them, as a lunar rainbow.

One of the results of the transformation was that great masses of crag had fallen, and a mightier mass than all hung trembling in a black abyss. As soon as the sky had cleared Old Mould was abroad on the mountain, his bleared eyes greedily fixed on the loosened crag. His tottering mind saw in the wet, glowing ironstone the realisation of his life-dream. The ruined speculators, the engineers, the miners—all were wrong. *His* faith in the mountain was fulfilled. As he looked, a cold perspiration broke over his body. He steadied himself as he sank on a boulder, and then in imagination took up two great handfuls of glistening gold, and let the bright coins run through his bony fingers. The parchment in the powder canister, ay, and more, more were his!

A shepherd and his dog passed close by, but Mould never saw them. He thought a while longer, then went down to his hut. He would blast the crag from the breast that held it, and if only the heart of the mountain confirmed what he suspected, then he was rich, rich indeed!

As the short afternoon fell he started off to cry "*Open Sesame.*" A barrel of gunpowder lay on his bare shoulder; and wrapped in his rough frieze coat was a delicate straw-stem fuse. *These* would solve the mystery!

They solved two mysteries,—a greater and a less.

The powder and fuse were placed in position. A flint and steel supplied a spark, and Mould's shambling legs carried him off over the rugged boulders. Then he watched,—watched for a red glare to tear the sky, and a thundering sound to shake the mountain. But neither came. Save for the hoarse croak of a raven and the bark of a fox, nothing broke the stillness.

One hour, two, three.

The fuse must have failed, or the powder have become damp; and as the moon and stars lit up the crags, Mould made as though to examine the spot. He gained it.

Precisely what happened next is not known. Suddenly it seemed as though the mountain had exploded. There was a terrible glare, something like an earthquake shook the ground, and thousands of tons of rock and *débris* rushed down into the White Quartz Valley.

That was all. The great, green mountain had taken Mould to her broader bosom, and the night wanderings of the old man had led him in the way of the Delectable Mountains whence there is no return.

IV.

After an hour's hard climbing we gain one of the topmost outliers, whence we command an extensive map-like view of the circumjacent mountains. A final struggle for the last ridge, and then along its crest. We are at an angle formed by the vales of Grasmere, Legberthwaite, and Patterdale, when a magnificent effect is produced as the sun suddenly pierces the clouds. A golden mass of molten sea stretches eastward. Bright sunny patches light up the landscape below; and a billowy sea of mountains rolls away, with every wave a name. Purple pavilions of hills stretch far and beyond on every side. Now we are among the clouds, and look down on all things mundane.

We "rush" the last slope, and at last stand

three thousand feet above sea level—upon the topmost jag of the mighty Helvellyn !

The grandeur of a mountain is always enhanced by a storm ; and as by the wave of a wizard's wand the sun is suddenly shut out by black, inky clouds. A couple of ominous ravens rise slowly uttering a dismal croak, croak, croak ; and a merlin rushes past on the wings of the storm. Mists gather, roll up the mountainside, and far-off mutterings are heard in the hills. As a cold plash strikes the face, we seek a cairn, drawing closer our wraps. Suddenly the storm bursts. In a moment we are soaked with blinding mist and chilled to the marrow. The storm lashes itself to a fury, and for a moment the grandeur is terrible and fascinating. It spends itself, passes as quickly as it came, and a glorious transformation is at hand.

Quivering lines of light shoot from the heavens, the sun bursts in all its strength, and Nature is a flood of dripping gold. The gauzy vapours disperse, and every grass-blade is draped and glowing with resplendent gems. A blue, foam-flushed sky displaces the sullen clouds, and the storm miracle is complete. Then we emerge from the dripping cairn to look abroad. That far, silvery streak, lying shimmering and blue, is Windermere. Directly south Esthwaite Water, whilst Coniston, with its pine-clad slopes, lies to the west. Ulleswater is at our feet, and

Red Tarn, black and silent, below. Striding Edge is the spot where young Gough was killed. To its north-west is Swirrel Edge. That is Catchedecam. Betwixt the last-named and Saddle-back a bit of the Solway is seen; while the skyline beyond is formed by the Scotch mountains. The ravines and precipices of the sides of Helvellyn exemplify in a striking manner the possible power of those elements whose ordinary effects are trivial and unnoticed.

A mountain storm in summer is terrible enough if long continued; but the same phenomenon in winter is grander and more terrible still. The crags of the English mountains claim a long list of victims; but for tragic interest the following is perhaps the saddest of all. The subject of it was a young man of great promise, who in early life had been educated for the Church. Just as he was ripe for college, his father, who was at the head of a great mercantile concern, died. This event made it imperative that the young scholar should immediately embark in trade—an undertaking as uncongenial as imperative. The fortunes of his family were threatened, and the only hope of his mother and sisters was that the son should successfully carry on what the father had commenced. A student of books rather than of men, he was ill fitted for the unequal fight, and after struggling for ten years was only liberated by ruin. His brother it is said, made him a bankrupt. "The din of populous cities had long stunned his brain, and his soul had sickened in the presence of the money-hunting eyes of selfish men, all madly pursuing their multifarious machinations in the great mart of commerce. The very sheeted masts of ships, bearing the flags of foreign countries, in all their pomp and beauty sailing homeward or outward bound, had become hateful to his spirit—for what were they but the floating enginery of Mammon? Truth, integrity, honour, were all recklessly sacrificed to gain by the friends he loved and had respected most—sacrificed without shame and without remorse—repentance being with them a repentance only over ill-laid schemes of villainy—plans for the ruination of widows and orphans—blasted in the bud of their iniquity." Following upon the loss of worldly fortune Gough's mother died, and had it not been for a legacy which came to him about this time he would have been absolutely penniless. A relative had died abroad—almost his only one, and the last of his name. Upon his small means he determined to seek an asylum among the northern mountains, where he might study nature and daily stand face to face with her most majestic forms and moods. He left the city which had wrought his ruin at midnight, the last definite object which his eyes rested upon being his mother's grave. The graveyard which contained it lay hard by one of the great arteries of life, and the roar of its myriad sounds was absent neither night nor day. A myriad graves were matted and massed together—a dank, unlovely sight, and one which invested death only with its worst and darkest attributes.

As late winter passed into spring, Gough took up his abode with the family of a northern yeoman in a Westmorland cottage. The majesty of the mountains on this first spring day deeply impressed the city-bred man, and his solitary life among the hills was begun with much heartfelt meditation. The mighty Helvellyn stood out boldly, its crest sharply etched against the sky. Even in this remote spot the wanderer wished to withdraw himself for a time wholly from the eyes of men; and as he gazed upon the passionless peak he thought that there he should be alone—there find solitude. As the short afternoon fell he started to make the rugged ascent. Every shoulder of the mountain gained put him farther beyond human aid, and each look at the peaceful valley below was nearer his last. Still he progressed. The keen air, the first deep inspiration of a purer joy—these lured him on. The face of the sky changed, but he saw it not. Its little lot of stars came out over the mountain, and, oblivious of the fact that night was at hand, he hurried on. The crescent moon rose and floated over its reflection in Red Tarn; and now the wanderer has reached the topmost, silent peak. Steeped in softest moonlight, he looked on the wondrous world below, and saw an English sight such as man has rarely seen. In the delirium of a new bliss the mountain "looked lovelier than dreamland in the reflected glimmer of the snow; and thus had midnight found him, in a place so utterly lonesome in its remoteness from all habitations, that even in summer no stranger sought it without the guidance of some shepherd."

Rising from the stone on which he sat, a flake of snow touched his face, then another, and another. He ran rapidly down the first slope, struck the path, and hurried on. The light was quickly fading. The moon was hidden, and the tarn, which but a moment before lay at his feet, had gone out. Neither road nor path was now visible, and the poor pilgrim of nature, utterly bewildered, plunged blindly into the almost inextricable passes of the mountains. The snow fell thicker and thicker, and as the storm rose it was swept hither and thither in blinding banks and opaque masses until every familiar object was hidden. Although almost overcome with the lashing and fury of the storm the traveller in wildest desperation staggered on, until an awful precipice for ever put a cruel end to his wanderings. . . . .

Snow-lines are sketched along the fences of the fells, but this is all that remains. Everything out of doors testifies to the coming of spring, and green grass-shoots are everywhere. The foaming fell "becks" sparkle in the sun, and the sheep are sprinkled over the crags. A breadth of blue is overhead, and the feeding flock is steadily turned towards the sky-line. This is the first token of the short summer, and all the sheep on all the hills rejoice. It is at this season that the shepherds most keenly scan their flocks and note the ravages of winter. By the torrent side, by the leas of the boulders, along the rock ledges—everywhere is dotted a white fleece.

It was upon such an occasion, the snow having melted, that a shepherd on his rounds came suddenly upon a dog which emerged from a bracken and boulder-strewn brae. The poor creature was reduced almost to a skeleton, and upon the man following, it whined and ran forward. It stopped over a weathered corpse—the body of young Gough, beside which it had kept watch and ward for months. It would allow no one to come near, though it was noticed that its collar bore a name—the name of its master, and that which established his identity. In the absence of the dog on its food forays the hill foxes, ravens, and buzzards had done their carnage on the body. This was taken by a party of yeomen and shepherds and interred in the burial ground of the Friends' Meeting House at Tirrel.

Both Scott and Wordsworth have fittingly commemorated the incident, though the lines are too well known to be quoted here.

CHAPTER XIII.

WORKERS IN WOODCRAFT.

I.

THE gamekeeper's cottage stands at the end of the oak lane. An orchard surrounds his dwelling, the brown boughs now drooping with ripened fruit. Under an overhanging sycamore is a kennel of silky-coated setters and a brace of spaniels. The former have beautifully-domed heads and large soft eyes. The spaniels with their pendulous ears are a black and a brown. Pheasant pens are scattered about the orchard, each containing half-a-dozen birds. In a disused shed are traps for taking game, and nets and snares found in rabbit runs or taken from poachers. The keeper does not always take these engines when he finds them, but waits quietly until they are visited by the "moucher;" then he makes a double capture. Few of the poachers, however, leave their traps after dark, and only the casual is caught in this way. At the other end of the orchard divisional boxes are ranged round an old barn-like building where pheasants' eggs are hatched. A shaggy terrier, with fresh mould upon its nose, peeps from beneath the shed doorway. Drowsy bluebottles buzz about the vermin larder, and under the apple-trees are straw-thatched hives. Contented pigeons coo and bask on the hot slates of the barn roof, and bird-sounds are everywhere. These blocks, upon which sit their falcons, act as a reminder of an old English sport fast passing away. These are merlins and peregrines, kept for a friend by the keeper, who is fond of hawking. The merlins can pull down partridges, while the peregrines are flown at larger game. No sport so exhilarating as falconry, none so fascinating.

The interior of the keeper's cottage is as characteristic as its surroundings. Here are guns of every description—from the old-fashioned fowling piece and matchlock to the ponderous duck-gun. Above the chimney-piece hangs a modern breechloader with Damascus barrels. The keeper admires the delicate mechanism of this, but deprecates the spirit of the age which produced it. Such cunningly-devised engines will make old-fashioned sport, or what he calls "wild shooting," extinct. By this he means the traversing of rough ground in healthful anticipation of a miscellaneous and always uncertain bag. It is this very uncertainty which gives the chief zest to sport. Against the walls are cases of stuffed birds, with a red squirrel or a white stoat to relieve the feathers. In one case a knot-hole is imitated from which peer three young weasels; and an old one is descending the hole with a dead bird in its mouth. All these are portrayed to the life by the keeper's own hand. Looking at the contents of the cases, he deplores his want of ornithological knowledge in earlier years. Among the stuffed specimens are a Greenland falcon, a pair of hobbies, several rare owls, swallow-tailed kite, hoopoe, rose-coloured pastor, and others equally rare.

The gamekeeper's life is essentially an outdoor one. He is far from populous towns, and needs but little assistance. Poachers rarely come to his preserves in gangs, and a couple of village mouchers he can easily manage. His powerful frame has once been the seat of great strength, though now it needs but a glance to show that his eye is less keen and his hand less firm. Still he is quick to detect, and with his hard-hitting muzzle-loader he rarely misses. Given favourable conditions he is almost infallible with the gun, though he gives his game law. He cannot now cover his extended ground in a single day, and perhaps does less night watching than formerly. His beat covers a widely diversified district with almost every species of game. The pheasants wander about the woods and copses; the partridge are among the corn and stubble; and rabbits pop in and out everywhere. Hares haunt the meadows and upland fields, and snipe go away from the marshes. Woodcock come to the wet woods, and a host of sea-haunting creatures feed along the bay. There is a heronry in the wood, and pigeons build in the larches. Of the habits of these creatures the keeper is full; and if he is garrulous he is always instructive. By observing, he has found that animals and birds have stated times and well-defined routes. Exactly at the same hour, according to the sun, the partridges and pheasants resort to the same spots. Hares follow the tracks day by day, and rooks fly morning and evening along the same valleys. Nightly, herons stalk the pools and the otter traces the mountain burns to their source. At noon a sparrow-hawk speeds by the covert, and at evening a kestrel hangs over the rickyard. In the afternoon, regularly, weasels run along the old wall; and as these things the flowers in their times of opening and closing are not less constant.

The keeper's domain encloses a park in which are red deer and fallow. Sometimes he has to shoot a fawn for the " great house." This he singles out, hitting it if possible just behind the shoulder. In season he must provide a certain "head" of game. Twice weekly he procures this, and takes it to the hall. For its proper hanging in the larder he is responsible. When the keeper wants game he knows to a yard where it may be found—where the birds will get up and in what direction they will go away. If a hare, he knows the gate or smoot through which it will pass, and out of this latter fact he makes capital. It is well known to poachers that when once a hare has been netted there is no chance of its being taken again in like manner. Rather than go through a second time, even though a "lurcher" be but a yard behind, it will either "buck" the gate or take the fence. Consequently the keeper has netted every hare on his ground. This greatly reduces the poacher's chances, and wire snares are now the only engines that can be successfully used. Spring and summer are taken up with breeding and rearing pheasants, and this is an anxious time. The work is not difficult but arduous. And then so much of the keeper's work is estimated by the head of game he can turn out. This result is tangible, and one that can be seen by both his master and visitors. There is nothing to show for long and often fruitless night-watching but rheumatism; and so the keeper appreciates all the more readily the praise accorded him for the number of well-grown birds he can show at the covert side. After pheasant-shooting in October the serious winter work of the keeper begins. Each week he has to kill from three to five hundred rabbits, which are sent to the markets of the large manufacturing towns. He can employ what engines against them he pleases, but the number must be produced. Firing a hundred shots a day is now more jarring than it was once; it has made him slightly deaf, and he adopts other means of destruction. He works the warrens in winter, but long waiting for a glutted ferret in frost and snow is not pleasant. Under favourable conditions, however, a great many rabbits may be taken in this way. Iron spring traps are used in the rabbit tracks, but these are impracticable on a large scale; and the pheasants and partridges, which run much, are apt to be caught in them. Moreover it is now illegal to set these traps in the open. The most certain and wholesale method of capture is by the "well-trap." This is a pit, placed immediately opposite to a hole in the fence through which the rabbits run from the woods to the field or pasture. Through the "run" a wooden trough is inserted, and as the rabbits pass through the floor opens beneath their weight and they drop into the "well." Immediately the pressure is removed the floor springs back to its original position; and thus a score or more rabbits may often be taken in a single night. In the construction of these traps rough and unbarked wood is used, and even then the rabbits will not take them for weeks. Then they become familiar, the weather washes away all scent, and the "well-trap" is a wholesale engine of capture. The rabbits of course are taken alive. These the keeper stretches across his knee, dislocating the spine. English rabbits are degenerating in size, and the introduction of some of the continental varieties would be beneficial. With the rabbits in autumn great quantities of wood-pigeons are sent away, the birds at this time becoming exceedingly plump and fat. An almost incredible number of acorns may be found in the crop of a single bird when the former have fallen.

These are a few of the keeper's duties. He himself has a russet, weather-beaten face, bounded by silvery hair. He might stand for a picture of a highly-idealised member of his class. So secluded is his cottage that he locks the door but once a year, and that on Christmas Eve. He can remember when there was larger game than now, when badgers and wild cats were not uncommon. One of his ancestors was an inveterate deer-stealer, as the parish books show. Then the red-deer roamed almost wild on the fells. To-day he has but one regret—that he was not contemporary with the wolf, the wild boar, and the bear. Of these in Britain he has just read an account, together with the vast primitive forests through which they roamed.

II.

THE CHARCOAL BURNERS.

The humid climate of the north-west of England is peculiarly favourable to the growth of coppice-wood; and scattered along the slopes of the valleys copses prevail, consisting for the most part of oak, ash, birch, and hazel. This growth beautifully clothes the hill-slopes, and in addition to taking away the bareness, brings to them much animal and bird life; and besides this, the young timber is fairly remunerative. The coppice woods are cut every fifteen years, and the ground set apart to it pays about equal to that devoted to grazing. This is owing to the fact that every part of the wood is well suited to some particular use, and finds a ready market. What these uses are will be presently seen.

As to the beauty and well-woodedness which the copses give to the north-west valleys there can be no question; and that life abounds in them which was foreign to the bare Fells is made equally clear by traversing them at almost any season of the year. Shelter they give, too, which is always important in districts subject to mountain storms. Metallic-lustred and brightly-coloured lichens light up the floor of the wood, the rabbits rustle through; innumerable birds are there, and dormice hang their ball-like nests among the hazel boughs. As the coppice grows the squirrel comes to the nuts, wood pigeons coo, and jays screech in the glades. Even a few pheasants have wandered here, and an occasional woodcock breeds among the dead oak leaves.

Just as the kindly sheltering woods have brought birds which are foreign to the district, so they have brought human settlers, and standing above on the bare Common we see rising from the trees columns of pale blue smoke. In the primitive cottages from whence these come reside the charcoal burners. Men they are whose lives glide on almost without influence from the outside world—quiet workers of many virtues. They observe well times and seasons, are full of country proverbs, wise as to signs of wind and weather, and draw deductions from the nature around them. Their occupation is such as keeps them in the woods for months at a spell, not even leaving them on Sundays. And so it comes that the decay of the black bryony berries and the rustle of the dead oak leaves have lessons for them; and as the winds of autumn sough through the bare branches, they are conscious that a time will come when they too must pass away. Piety in men so lived may seem strange, but when a man stands face to face with nature, by far the best elements of his nature are developed. He is brought, as it were, back to his primitive life, and is more a man than the dweller in towns.

During the summer we have tramped through the coppice woods. These will be felled when autumn comes round, having grown their fifteen years. And to one unaccustomed to such rapid growth the progress made would be somewhat astonishing. The trees are spindle high. The ash-poles are straight and smooth, the young oaks radiant in rich chestnut, the hazels catkin-covered, and the frail birch—the lady of the woods—towers her silvery stem afar up. Of course, when cut, each species of tree has some special virtue—some quality in which it most excels. The young oaks, for instance, are felled at the time of ascending sap in early summer, as then the bark is easily "peeled." This is extensively used in the process of tanning. The torn staves are used in making baskets and hoops. The "afflictive birch, cursed by unlettered idle youth," has other uses than that which the quotation would seem likely to imply. The variously sized boughs are used in making crates, and the wood is also extensively used by the cottagers as fire "eldin," which may be detected when in proximity to the cottages. The use, however, to which the majority of the wood is put is bobbin-turning—quite an extensive and important industry in the northern valleys.

The enemies of the trees, and the only ones which stop their growth, are two. Insects with their borings, and rabbits. The latter, in severe winters, eat the bark of the young trees to a surprising height from the ground, and by so doing impede their growth.

The second industry to which the coppice woods give rise, and by far the most interesting, is the charcoal burning, almost peculiar to this part of the country. We shall detail it as practised in the extensive Honeybee Woods. At the felling of the copse the wood is roughly divided into two "sets." The thick upright poles, of whatever tree, are stacked for "bobbin wood," and the thinner parts await the charcoal burners. These are also the men that from autumn to spring are busily employed in cutting, stacking, and arranging the wood.

The first months of spring are employed in peeling the oak for its bark, and from early summer into autumn the actual charcoal burning is done. The men who take part in the lonely trade live in rude huts in the woods, thatched with heather and bracken. Heaps of dried ferns serve them for beds, and their wants are few. Their huts are fixed first as to shelter and the presence of water, then with regard to proximity to their labours. From this ground they are never absent, the burning wood heaps requiring constant attention and aid from a quick eye as to change of wind and the coming of rain. The burning is conducted as follows: The faggots (from one to four feet in length and about one and a half inches thick) are built up round a vertical stake, which forms the centre of the mass, until the heap has attained considerable dimensions. It is round, and represents a low stack terminating in an apex at the top. When sufficient faggots have been piled up, the whole is covered with turf and wet sand, so as to exclude the air. The heap, now about thirty feet in diameter, is flattened by beating with spades, and made to present a smooth dome-like surface. The vertical stake is withdrawn from the centre, and lights are dropped down the passage left, to ignite the wood. The air has been carefully excluded so as to regulate the burning of the heap. From the centre the fire gradually spreads outwards until it reaches the edges. The burners always have in readiness large screens to regulate the supply of air, and these are planted on that side of the heap from which the wind blows. The screens consist of wooden hurdles intertwined with dead grass, dried fern, and bracken. Of course success depends upon the slow and equal burning of the whole mass. A shifting wind sometimes ill regulates the supply of air and fires the heap. When this occurs nothing can stop it, and the charcoal is completely spoiled. This, however, from the great watchfulness of the men, is generally avoided. To return to the heap. The products of combustion escape by the channel occasioned by the withdrawal of the vertical stake. The process is continued from twenty to thirty hours, when smoke and fumes seem to come off every part alike. This is a sign to put out the fire, which is done by applying water. The faggots have now been converted into charcoal. The critical part of the operation, and the one that wants most experience, is to catch the heap when it is "enough"—that is when it is neither overdone nor underdone. After allowing half a day for cooling, the charcoal is taken out, put into sacks, and carted away. Three or four men generally work together and have four heaps in hand at one time. At night, especially when there is much wind, the burners work by shifts. The charcoal when carted away is just half the weight of the wood from which it has been prepared. Much of the charcoal prepared hereabouts is used in smelting at the Backbarrow and other neighbouring ironworks. Iron so smelted is of much higher commercial value than that obtained by the ordinary processes. Charcoal burning, consequently, is likely to continue a lucrative employment for many years to come, especially as coppice woods—the raw material—thrive so abundantly in the district.

To watch these men at their lonely employment in the woods is well worth a visit. They and their work are alike interesting, and the woods · which provide their employment are fascinating at all seasons. A nearer acquaintance with the workers will reveal the fact that they know the "herbs and simples of the woods," and also much of the contents of an old "herbal" lying in the hut. In the virtues of plants they have great belief, and can tell of interesting traits in the life-history of wild flowers. We believe, too, that they exercise "free right and warren" of the woods where they reside, and of this no one seems to care to deprive them. They are pleasant, primitive fellows wonderfully intelligent as to out-door questions, and command the respect of every one with whom they come in contact. We might have said that their necessary victuals are supplied periodically from the outside world, but in domestic matters they do all things for themselves.

III.

THE FORESTER.

Walking in the woods, we met the old man standing over the prostrate form of a fallen monster that had been uprooted by the wind. He was about to lop off the branches, and was trimming the bole with an axe. The tree had brought several others with it of younger growth, and he had just finished clearing to obtain a space wherein to work. Black bryony berries were twined about the lower branches, as were the dead leaves of honeysuckle. These are among the natural enemies of the old man, as he considers them injurious to timber. His woods are wide, and constitute his little world. There is little in or of them which he does not know, even to the flowers and birds. For these he has quaint provincial names of his own. Thus he speaks of the fallowchat, the nettle-creeper, and the reed-wren—meaning the wheatear, white-throat, and reed-warbler. The frail anemone he knows as the wind-flower, coltsfoot is one of his rustic remedies for coughs, and the early purple orchids are to him "crow's feet." His "little red mouse that rustles among the dead leaves and is coloured like a hare" is our wood-mouse; and sometimes he finds among the hazel branches the ball-like nests of the dormice. He knows that wherever fungi grows there is death, and the tree lighted up by the brightly-coloured bosses he marks with a red cross, which is as signing the warrant of its doom. He follows the yaffle, and wherever it pecks the trees he knows that decay has begun within. This applies to all the woodpeckers, who are infallible valuers of growing timber, and all trees which they attack are marked out for the axe. Often on the outside the boles are apparently sound, and it is hard to believe that the heart-wood is decayed; but the winged wood-prophets never err.

It matters not what living thing crosses our path, the old man names it, even to the insects. He tells how these are instrumental in producing the oak-galls, and points out the insidious attacks and borings of weevils. Of all trees the elm has most enemies. He tears off a bit of bark from a still growing tree, and reveals a labyrinth of channels radiating on two sides from a central line. The *Scolytus* he simply calls "elm-borer," though from his conversation it is plain that he is a close observer, and knows the whole life-history of the insect. And thus, in addition to his special knowledge of woodcraft, he knows the time of the coming of the birds, of the retiring of the insect hosts, and the habitats of the flowers.

The woodman lives in a stone hut, near the confines of what was once an extensive forest, through which trooped vast herds of deer, both red and fallow. His weather-beaten face, which in colour resembles a ripe russet apple, tells of long exposure to summer's sun and winter's cold. His hair is white, and his form as yet but slightly bowed. The only other occupant of the hut is a girl grandchild, who has long lived with him. Neither have ever been more than a dozen miles from the spot, nor care to. Nominally the old man's work is to look after the woods of one valley. This has been his life-work, and he has no longing for change. He knows nothing of what goes on without a narrow circle, and his Bible and an occasional country newspaper constitute his sole literature.

As becomes his craft he never tires of talking of trees. In his woods the giant oak is common, with its gnarled and twisted bole, its wildly reticulated branches, its lichens, and its host of insect visitors. He has himself detected the two varieties of the oak, and points out the difference. In one case the acorns are borne on stalks, in the other they are sessile. Of these he speaks as the long and short-stalked kinds. He has no confidence in the popular theory that the wood of the one greatly excels that of the other. He has worked both, and has not discovered any substantial difference. In late autumn he gathers from beneath the oaks huge sacksful of acorns, of which he disposes to the farmers. Next comes the majestic beech, with its smooth bole and olive-grey bark. The old man recalls its wondrous flood of green in spring, and its not less glorious gold in autumn.

Some modern Orlando even haunts the forest

hereabouts, and abuses the young trees with carving not Rosalind but "Emilie" on their barks. The sentiment which stops the growth of the young beeches appeals to no finer sense within the bosom of the old man. And so he roundly denounces the wandering lover who has carved thereon the name he adores, in no unmeasured terms.

In summer a few purple beeches light up the wood, and the old man is surprised to learn that all trees of this variety sprang from a single tree which was found growing wild in the midst of one of the immense forests of Thuringia. But more than all the interest that attaches to the trees are the uses to which their wood is put. The little church on the Fellside opposite consists internally of oak from this very wood; and so, too, do half the beams and rafters in the parish. The hard, close-grained wood of the beech, too, is used for a great variety of purposes as well as fuel. Interspersed throughout the wood are numbers of ash-trees, soon to be arrayed in feathery lightness, but now more reminding us of Tennyson's naturalistic simile, "Black as ashbuds in March." The toughness and elasticity of the wood of the ash are well known, and here is an opportunity for the display of the timber genius of our old friend. There is, he tells us, little else than this about the yard of the village wheelwright. Cart shafts are made from it, as are the primitive agricultural implements used in the valley; of like wood is his own axe handle and spade shaft. In the country infinite almost are the uses of the ash.

In the middle of the wood, and coming down to the stream sides, are a retinue of fringed elms, both Campestris and Montana. Some of these have attained to an immense size, and are at one with the scenery. But in the open spots of the wood—in the glades where life most prevails—are the beautiful birches, with their striped, silvery bark. Well does this tree merit its appellation of "lady of the woods." There is none so frail, so graceful, nor so generally beautiful. Almost every part of the birch is used and for a great variety of purposes. In spring the delicate green of the larch hangs in trailing tassels, and contrasts well with the dark green foliage of the indigenous pine. The old forester has an "Unter den Linden" equal, at least in beauty, to any in Europe, and in summer the trees are a veritable haunt of summer wings. The field maple and the sycamore are here, and interspersed in the open spaces a few white stemmed walnuts. These in autumn yield a rich harvest to the forester. The horse-chestnut is common, and then come a host of trees of minor growth. All the wild fruit trees are here, and hang out glories of snowy and pink blossoms in spring—the pear, the cherry, and the wild apple. Sombre yews that set off the pale green of the woodlands are plentiful, and in them the cushats and the jays build. In addition to these there are the wild service tree, white beam, and mountain ash, the last called by the old man the rowan.

Planting and thinning and felling constitute the work of the woodman throughout the year. But there are a thousand little offshoots of woodcraft of which he has knowledge and which he indulges at times. Like the charcoal burners, he holds free right and warren of the woods. He can make many primitive lures for taking wild creatures, and is an adept at "gins" and "springs" for destroying vermin. In winter he sets snares for woodcock and snipe. He is a great favourite with the resident boys at the neighbouring grammar school, and procures them mice and squirrels and birds' eggs. He makes wooden pegs and teeth for the farmers, and various little articles for the farm women. He sells bundles of faggots and sticks for supporting peas, and a dozen other perquisites, all products of the woodlands. The embrowned nuts of autumn he turns to profitable account. In the forest are numerous hazel copses, together forming many acres. In autumn the old man was surprised to receive a visit from a burly man in a gig. He told the woodman, in a dialect differing from his own, that he was a "badger;" and then and there made an astounding bid for the nuts. The old man closed with the handsome offer, and this sum now adds annually to his otherwise slight income.

CHAPTER XIV.

SKETCHES FROM NATURE.

I.

NATURE'S WEATHER PROPHETS.

NATURE'S barometers are the only ones of which most country-folk have any knowledge. These they may consult at all times, and they know them by heart. Almost all field-workers are "weather wise," and their conversation on this head has no town conventionalism about it. The farmer has been so beaten about by wind and weather that he himself is scarcely sensible to changing atmospheric conditions; but that does not prevent his observing its influence on the things about him. Before rain his dogs grow sleepy and dull, the cat constantly licks herself; geese gaggle in the pond, fowls and pigeons go early to roost, and the farm horses grow restless. Abroad, the ants are all hurry and scurry, rushing hither and thither; spiders crowd on the wall; toads emerge from their holes; and the garden paths are everywhere covered with slugs and snails. When the chaffinch says "weet, weet," it is an infallible sign of rain. As the rain draws nearer peacocks cry and frogs croak clamorously from the ditches. These are signs which almost every one has heard who lives in the country; though one of the surest ways of predicting weather changes is by observing the habits of snails. Snails never drink, but imbibe moisture during rain and exude it afterwards. They are seldom seen abroad except before rain, when they commence climbing trees and getting upon leaves. The tree snail is so sensitive to weather that it will commence to climb two days before the rain comes. If the downpour is to be prolonged, the snail seeks the under part of a leaf; but if a short or light rain is coming on, it stays on the outside. There is another species which is yellow before and bluish after it. Others indicate change by dents and protuberances resembling tubercles. These begin to show themselves ten days before rain, and when it comes the pores of the tubercles open and draw in the moisture. In others again deep indentations, beginning at the head between the horns and ending with the jointure of the tail, appear a few days before a storm.

One of the simplest of nature's barometers is a spider's web. When there is a prospect of wind or rain, the spider shortens the filaments by which its web is sustained and leaves it in this state as long as the weather is variable. If it elongates its threads, it is a sign of fine calm weather, the duration of which may be judged by the length to which the threads are let out. If the spider remains inactive, it is a sign of rain; if it keeps at work during rain, the downpour will not last long, and will be followed by fine weather. Observation has taught that the spider makes changes in its web every twenty-four hours, and that if such changes are made in the evening, just before sunset, the night will be clear and beautiful.

Sleeping is characteristic of certain plants; and though it was at one time thought that this might have reference to the habits of insects, it is now believed to be more dependent on the weather. The tiny scarlet pimpernel, the "old man's weather-glass," opens at seven and closes soon after two. The daisy unfolds its flower at sunrise and sleeps at sunset. Dandelions close up at about five o'clock; at which time the white water-lily has been asleep an hour and the mouse-ear chickweed two hours. The yellow goat's-beard opens at four and closes just before twelve, and has for its English name "John-go-to-bed-at-noon." Local circumstance influences the flowers in their opening and closing, though they are pretty constant from day to day. Many flowers close their petals during rain—probably to prevent the honey and pollen from being rendered useless or washed away.

Birds are admirable weather prophets, and from their number and obtrusiveness have furnished many examples. In his "Paradise of Birds," Mr. Courthope makes one of them say—

> " Besides, it is true
>   To our wisdom is due
> The knowledge of Sciences all ;
> And chiefly those rare
>   Metaphysics of air
> Men ' Meteorology ' call.
>
> And men, in their words,
>   Acknowledge the Birds'
> Erudition in weather and star;
> For they say ' Twill be dry,
>   The swallow is high,'
> Or ' Rain, for the chough is afar.'"

Mr. Ruskin says that he was not aware of this last weather-sign ; nor, he supposes, was the Duke of Hamilton's keeper, who shot the last pair of choughs on Arran in 1863. He trusts that the climate has wept for them, and is certain that the Coniston clouds grow heavier in these his last years. All the birds of the swallow kind fly high at the advent of or during fine weather, and low before a storm. These facts are accounted for by another. When the weather is calm the ephemeræ upon which swallows feed fly high in air, but just over the earth or water if it be rough. The cry of the chaffinch has already been mentioned; in Scotland the children say, "Weet-weet [the cry], Dreep-dreep" [the consequence].

In Hampshire swans are believed to be hatched in thunderstorms; and it is said that those on the Thames have an instinctive prescience of floods. Before heavy rains they raise their nests. This is characteristic of many birds, which add piles of material to their nests to prevent swamping. When rooks fly high, and seem to imitate birds of prey by soaring, swooping, and falling, it is an almost certain sign of coming storms. Staying in the vicinity of the rookery, returning at midday, or coming to roost in groups, are also said to be omens to the like effect. Various proverbs would seem to indicate that the cry of the owl, heard in bad weather, foretells a change. The constant iteration of the green woodpecker's cry before a storm has given it the name of rain-bird, rain-pie, and rain-fowl. Storm-cock is a provincial name shared by this bird and the missel-thrush, the latter often singing through gales of wind and rain. Storm-bird is also applied to the fieldfare. The abhorrence in which the mariners hold the swallow-like storm-petrel is well known; its appearance is believed to denote wild weather. This little bird is the Mother Carey's chicken of sailors, and is also called storm-finch and water-witch. Herons, says an old author, flying up and down in the evening, as if doubtful where to rest, "presage some evill approaching weather"—a legend as old as Virgil, though probably devoid of foundation. Concerning gulls in general, children who live by the sea say "Seagull, seagull, sit on the sand; It's never good weather while you're on the land;" and fisherfolk know that when the seamews fly out early and far to seaward fair weather may be expected. To Scotch shepherds the drumming of snipe indicates dry weather and frost at night; and Gilbert White remarks that woodcocks have been observed to be remarkably listless against snowy foul weather; while, according to another author, their early arrival and continuance "foretells a liberal harvest." In Wiltshire the coming of the dotterel betokens frost and snow, and there is a proverb that the booming of the bittern will be followed by rain or worse. In Morayshire, when the wild geese go out to sea they say the weather will be fine; but if towards the hill, stormy. The saw-like note of the great titmouse is said to foretell rain; that of the blue-tit, cold. In the south of France so much store is set by the wisdom of the magpie, that if it builds its nest on the summit of a tree the country-folk expect a season of calm; but if lower down, winds and tempests are sure to follow. When a jackdaw is seen to stand on one of the vanes of the cathedral tower at Wells, it is said that rain is sure to follow within twenty-four hours. Wells must be a wet place! In Germany, dwellers in the country lack faith in the skylark's song as announcing fine weather; but when the lark and the cuckoo sing together they know that summer has come. The robin, buzzard, lapwing, starling, and a number of other birds are said to foretell weather changes.

We have, however, noticed that in nearly all the species named the various cries and calls are closely connected with the bird's food supply.

II.

FERRETS AND FERRETING.

The ferret commonly used in this country is an animal of the weasel kind, belonging to a large genus and having its true home in the Tropics. Unlike its British congeners, it shows its southern nature in being unable to stand any great degree of cold, even an English winter being sufficient to kill it if not properly housed. This may also be seen in rather a remarkable manner, as probably no one ever saw a ferret enter a rabbit-hole without its peculiar "shiver." Like the cat, it has a decided objection to wetting its fur, and especially does it show this upon being transferred from a warm pocket or bag to the damp soil of a burrow. Zoologically the ferret is one of the most interesting animals of the group to which it belongs; and this from the fact that it is a true breeding albino, having the white fur and pink eyes peculiar to this variety. Under domestication it breeds more frequently and is more prolific than in its wild state. It is somewhat smaller than the polecat, but readily breeds with that animal, and produces young intermediate in character between the parent species. It is owing to this fact that we have now two well-defined varieties—one of a brown colour, and known as the polecat ferret, the other the more common white variety. The first is said to be the more hardy and vicious; and it is to secure these qualities that keepers on large warrens cross their ferrets with the wild polecat.

In this country ferrets are kept more for work than as pets, and are used for making rabbits bolt from their burrows. To do this scarcely any training is necessary, and three young ferrets which we used the other day worked as well as their more experienced parents. There are various reasons why white ferrets are to be preferred as opposed to the brown polecat variety. They are usually more docile and pleasant to handle. A brown ferret is apt to be nipped up by a sharp dog in mistake for a rat or rabbit, while a white one is always apparent, even when moving amongst the densest herbage. This specially applies to night time, and hence poachers invariably use white ferrets. Gamekeepers who know their business prefer ferrets taken from poachers to any other. The poacher carefully selects his ferrets, and from the nature of his trade he cannot afford to work bad ones. Some ferrets cause rabbits to bolt rapidly, while others are slow. Sometimes a ferret will drive a rabbit to the end of a blind burrow, and after killing it will not return until it has gorged itself with blood; and more trouble is added if the ferret curls itself up for an after-dinner sleep. Then of course it has either to be left or dug out; if the former, it is well to bar every exit and to return with a dead rabbit when hunger has succeeded the gorged sleep. Ferreting is mostly practised in winter; and it is to guard against such occasions as these that working ferrets are generally muzzled. A cruel practice used to obtain of stitching together the lips of ferrets to prevent their worrying rabbits and then "laying up." But the most humane method of muzzling is with soft string; a muzzle constructed of which may be quite effective and at the same time not uncomfortable to wear. Care must be taken not to hurt the ferret, as if the string annoys him he will do nothing but endeavour to get it off. Occasionally ferrets are worked with a line attached; but this is an objectionable practice. There may be a root or stick in which the line may get entangled, when there will be digging, and no end of trouble in getting it out.

From what has been already said, and from the uncertainty of ferreting, it will be understood why the poacher can only afford to use the best animals. Of the many modes of taking the "coney," ferreting is the most common. Of course this is the poacher's method; but it varies little from that of the gamekeeper or the legitimate "sportsman." When the rabbits can be induced to bolt freely very good sport can be had; but in this respect they are most capricious. They bolt best on a windy day and before noon; after that they are sluggish, and often refuse to come out at all. As the rabbit "darts across a narrow ride like a little brown shadow, quick must be the eye and ready the hand that can get the gun to the shoulder and discharge it in the brief second that elapses between the appearance of a tiny brown nose on one side the path and the vanishing of a little snow-white patch of down on the other." Those that have ferreted much have probably seen strange revelations while indulging in the sport. A mound or brae sometimes seems to explode with rabbits, so wildly do they fly before their enemy. We have seen twenty rabbits driven from one set of holes. When the ferrets are running the burrows, stoats and weasels are occasionally driven out;

and among other creatures unearthed we remember a brown owl, a stock-dove, and a shell-duck, all of which were breeding in the mounds.

To many persons ferrets are objectionable pets; but if properly kept they are among the cleanest of animals. Playful as kittens, they are harmless if properly handled, and much fondling tendsto tame them. Ferrets not only soon get used to handling, but like it. They ought always to be seized boldly and without hesitation, for if the hold has to be adjusted a bite may be the result. And a bite from a ferret, especially to a person in bad health, is sometimes a serious matter. If a ferret is inclined to be vicious attract its attention with a glove in front, bringing the other hand down with a rapid sweep, grasping it firmly by the neck and shoulders. Food has much to do with temper, and confined under favourable conditions ferrets will be cleanly and sweet as in their natural habitat. They require to lie dry and have a roomy abode. Pine shavings are better than straw to bed them, and pine sawdust ought to be sprinkled about. The resinous matter in these acts as an antiseptic, and as a deterrent to vermin. Closely-confined ferrets become weak and tender, and are susceptible to cold. Bread and milk ought to be the prevailing food, with a good meal of flesh weekly. These combined will keep them in good condition and perfect health. The common diseases to which ferrets are liable are owing to unsuitable food and damp or dirty housing.

III.

OUR HERONRY.

The herons have just returned to the heronry after an absence of many months. At the end of September the old and young birds flew off together, and dispersed themselves over the lowlying mosses which margin the estuary of the river. Here they stayed during the winter, feeding but little in the bay, but making long flights either to the quiet tarns among the hills or to the neighbouring trout streams. Like the poacher, the heron pursues its silent trade by night, and loves the moonlit ones best. Now that the birds are breeding, their habit and daily routine are ordered quite otherwise than during the winter months. This year they returned to nest during the last week of March, and immediately sought out the trees in the most elevated part of the wood. By the middle of April but few nests remained unfinished, while the majority contained eggs. The trees selected for the huge burdens of sticks are oak, ash, elm, and silver firs; and the nests themselves are flat platforms with just the slightest depression for the pale green eggs. Close by the home of the herons is a rookery; and although it has not always been so, the two species now dwell together in perfect amity. Nests of the herons and of their sable companions are not unfrequently found in the same tree. Any threatened invasion of the two colonies of brooding birds produces a very different result on their respective denizens. The rooks get off their nests and circle, crying and cawing, until the disturber has vanished; the herons fly silently and straight away. During a stormy spring like the present * many of the eggs are blown from the nest and destroyed—a fate which often befalls the young herons themselves in autumn. Now that the birds are breeding it is easy to see by the aid of a binocular that they sit upon their nests with their legs under them, and not (as was once supposed) either pushed through the sticks or thrust behind them. In its domestic relations the heron is both amicable and honest. If a nest is blown down the birds go to work in the precincts of the rookery, but never touch the rooks' sticks. The heron's nest is a rude, widespreading platform constructed of beech-twigs, and not lined with wool as generally stated, but with the fine shoots of the larch. The appearance is that of a ringdove's nest on a large scale, and so open in texture that the sitting bird or eggs may be seen through the foundation. The

* 1890.

heron breeds both early and late, and has often three or four broods in a season. At this time they are rarely seen fishing in the bay, and seem to prefer round fish upon which to feed their young, probably on account of the narrowness of gape and swallow. To obtain the requisite food the herons move off at evening to the quiet tarns and streams which abound in trout and eels. As the young birds come to maturity they are driven from the nest, and in a few days a new clutch of eggs is laid. The incubation of these is performed by both parents, one sitting during the day the other at night. As soon as young herons are able to look about them they have a habit of standing erect in the nest, and, not being very stable, are not unfrequently blown to the ground. If no harm befalls them, they are here fed by the old birds, though they never attempt to regain their lofty nests. Everywhere beneath the heronry there is an ancient and fish-like smell; and this by the warm days of summer becomes almost unbearable.

When nesting operations are over, they leave their summer haunt among the tall trees and make down to the bay and low-lying marshes. At this season the birds are gregarious, and their daily movements afford material for pleasant study. If the fishing ground in the channel is fruitful, sport goes on harmoniously; but if otherwise, chase is given to the successful fishers by the lesser black-backed gulls; these birds invariably cause the herons to drop their game, catching it as it falls. See, on a calm sunny day in September, the Stacy-Marks-like group waiting patiently in the channel for the flow. Some are erect, with heads settled gracefully over their backs; others are exposing their breasts and outspread wings to the autumnal sun; while some few, like geese, may be seen settled on their legs with necks elegantly arched. It is not less interesting to watch an individual fisher than a group when the retiring tide has left the channel. It wades cautiously with lowered head and outstreched neck, each step being taken by a foot being drawn out of the water and as quietly replaced in advance. By gentle movements the heron is often enabled to strike and secure a flook at once. If a fish is missed, a sharp look-out is kept for its line of escape, and then a stealthy step is made in that direction. Should the distance be beyond reach of the bird's vision, a few flaps of the wings are tried in the eagerness of the pursuit. Sometimes a heron may be observed, when wading, to stand still suddenly, when no doubt its pectinated toe prevents the escape of a flat-fish or other victim.* A characteristic of flight may also be mentioned. When a heron rises from the ground the legs hang down, but as soon as it has acquired a settled flight

* Dr. T. Gough.

they are extended backwards. These and the retracted head and neck adjust the equipoise of the body. The slow languid flaps of the wings would seem to indicate the heron as a slow-flying bird ; but this impression is quite erroneous. If timed by a watch, it will be found that no fewer than two hundred and fifty separate wing movements are made per minute, counting the upward and downward strokes. The literary legacy as to the heron's varying altitude of flight foreboding fair weather or foul would seem to have no foundation in fact ; at least, years of observation have yielded no indication of this. The altitude of flight is regulated according to the distance of the bird's fishing ground. If the place is near, the flight is slow and sluggish at only a few yards above the surface ; if lower down the bay the flight is higher ; while if to a distant spot, more vigorous and rapid wing-movements indicate the intention.

When fishing in a trout stream the heron stands looking more like a lump of drift-stuff caught in the bushes than an animate object. Gaunt, consumptive, and sentinel-like, the bird watches with breast depressed and poised upon one leg. Woe to the tiny trout or samlet that comes within reach of its formidable pike, for it is at once impaled and gulped down. This impalement is given with great force, and a wounded heron has been known to drive its bill right through a stout stick. Nothing from fry to mature fish comes amiss to the heron, and the young consume great quantities. Sometimes they gaff an individual which is difficult to dispose of. It is related that a heron was seen one evening going off to a piece of water to feed ; the spot was visited next morning, when it was discovered that the bird had struck its beak through the head of an eel, and the eel thus held had coiled itself so tightly round the neck of the heron as to stop the bird's respiration, and both were found dead. An authoritative statement has been made to the effect that the heron's services in destroying pike, coarse fish, rats, and water-beetles may be set off against its depredations in trout streams ; but from this we must dissent.

IV

PLOVERS AND PLOVERS' EGGS.

In April and May thousands of plovers' eggs are annually sent to the London markets from all parts of the country. The *gourmets'* appreciation of this delicacy causes an ever-increasing demand, which, however rapid its growth, will always be met. For the green plover is one of the commonest of British birds, and is greatly on the increase. It flocks during the winter, and according to the severity or openness of the weather indulges in short local migrations from the plashy meadows and uplands to the sea-coast. Upon the approach of spring the flocks break up and resort to their breeding-grounds. These are usually at some elevation, and in the north the bird builds at an altitude of one thousand five hundred feet. Probably one of the reasons of the plover's great abundance is the readiness with which it adapts itself to local circumstance, and the clever manner in which it conforms to the environment in which it finds itself. For although a great many birds may be found breeding at a considerable elevation, numbers nest in the sea marshes, among the plough and upland fields, and along the marram-covered flats.

The lapwing is an early breeder, and eggs may often be found by the middle of March. It is these first captures which fetch such fancy prices in the market, and as much as fifteen shillings has been paid for a single egg. So anxious are the poulterers to obtain these, that one of them recently informed Mr. Howard Saunders that if he were assured of having the first ten eggs, he would not hesitate at giving five pounds for them. Of course, as the season advances the price rapidly decreases, and the normal price per dozen when the supply becomes general is about five shillings. As an instance of the difficulty which an untrained eye has in detecting the eggs of the green plover when in the nest, it may be mentioned that a person unaccustomed to birds'-nesting was sent up a furrow in which were six nests, each containing eggs, and these were to be collected. By the time that the end of the furrow was reached the collector had put his foot into one nest and had failed to find the other five. This is not always the case, however, and persons who study the habits of the plover experience but little difficulty in finding the nests. In fact, shepherds and others often walk straight up to them. They watch the movements of the parent bird, and know from the conformation of the ground to a yard where the nest will be. When you come upon a breeding haunt of green plovers, it will be noticed that many of the birds fly straight and silently away. When this is so it will be certain that the bird is the female and that it is sitting upon eggs. The bird does not rise immediately from the nest, but runs for a distance of some yards before it takes wing. If it allows a near approach, and rises low, the probability is that incubation is far advanced, and the eggs, of course, will not be worth taking. There are two ways, however, of determining this. Three or four eggs are the usual complement, and if there be fewer than three, or they are not warm to the hand, the bird has not begun to sit. Partly incubated eggs when placed in water float with their large end uppermost; if fresh

x

they sink on their sides. The conduct of the male is very different from that of his mate. If a person approach the nest, he flies crying and calling overhead, and tries to lure the intruder from the vicinity. His peculiarly rounded wings beat the air, causing a loud humming sound which in France has given to the lapwing its name of *vanneau*, a fan. One characteristic of birds of the plover kind is that they lay from three to four eggs; and this holds good with the lapwing. These are so well known as not to need description; but there is one peculiarity which may be remarked. The eggs are beautifully pyriform in shape, and when the female leaves the nest deliberately it will be found that the smaller ends of the eggs are together, thereby taking up but little room in the nest. When the young are hatched they run about immediately, often with the shell upon their backs. Although they must remain upon the ground for two or three weeks, they are admirably protected by the assimilative colouring of their down, which renders them most difficult to detect.

It would be interesting to know just when lapwings' eggs became a marketable commodity. Pennant as early as 1776 quotes them at three shillings a dozen; and thirty years later Daniel states that their price was four shillings. There would appear to be but little organisation in connection with the collecting of plovers' eggs, and this is probably why the price is kept up. The majority of the eggs are gathered by shepherds, keepers, and labourers, who are assisted by women and children; but the latter find comparatively few nests. Not unfrequently the early clutches are covered with snow, and more than one set of nests have been known to have perished in this way. But the species is a hardy one, and the birds persevere until they are successful in rearing one nest of young. Hence there is no ground for the apprehension expressed in some quarters lest so useful a bird (as this is stated to be to agriculturists) should be destroyed by taking a few of the first layings. That the peewit evinces considerable attachment to its nest and eggs the following example will show. On an evening about the middle of May a gentleman found a lapwing's nest containing four eggs. Three of these were completely covered with a cake of dry dung, which had accidentally been kicked over the nest by the cattle and which the birds were unable to remove. The eggs were chilled, but the gentleman took them home, placed them in an oven over-night, and at six next morning replaced them in the nest. The old birds were hovering about, and the hen went immediately to the nest. Three of the eggs hatched the following morning, the remaining one having been accidentally cracked.

It must not be supposed that all the so-called plovers' eggs exposed for sale have really been laid by that species. The eggs of rare wading birds have frequently been selected from among them, and those of the snipe are not at all uncommon. In cooking, it is discovered that numbers of eggs are far advanced in incubation, when, of course, they are useless; and it is not always easy to apply tests to determine this while purchasing. At table the eggs are usually served hard boiled. Sometimes they are shelled and served up with Béchamel sauce; though their more frequent use is as decoration for salad, the beautiful colour of the "white" admirably setting off the dish.

Not only are plovers' eggs delicacies, but some of the birds themselves are highly appreciated at table. Of all the species known to naturalists, however, two only are recognised by *gourmets*. These are the green and gold: the first the common kind, which produces the plovers' eggs; the second a handsome bird, somewhat rare, and larger than the former. It has beautiful golden markings, a soft liquid eye, and breeds upon the tops of the highest mountains. The golden plover fetches a much higher price than the green, and living the two are easily distinguishable. When cooked the difference in size is not appreciable, though the former may always be known by the absence of the hind-toe. Lapwings were formerly "mewed" for the purpose of feeding, and fatted upon liver. A thousand birds, supposed to be of this species, were served at a feast on the enthronisation of Archbishop Nevill. In Ireland the birds are netted in autumn in very considerable numbers; though, strangely enough, the eggs are neither appreciated nor collected as they are here. A new phase of the trade in lapwings' eggs is that of preserving them for use during the winter months.

v.

BROWN IN SUMMER, WHITE IN WINTER.

Of the protective colouring exhibited by several birds and quadrupeds in countries that remain during a greater part of the year under snow, Britain furnishes several interesting examples. Amongst these are the ptarmigan, variable or Alpine hare, ermine, Greenland falcon, snowy owl, Lapland bunting, with other less marked instances. The very existence of each of these creatures depends upon the closeness with which it conforms to its environment; and just as it does this effectively so it is robust as a species and flourishes. The inherent variability in some cases is great, and definite changes can be brought about in comparatively short periods. In other species, however, modification is slow, and only obtained by the long process of natural selection. As an instance of the first, we have the change from dark brown to purely white of the stoat or ermine; of the second, the indigenous red grouse of the British Isles is an example. This bird is found nowhere else in a wild state. With us there is no reason why it should assume the white winter plumage like its congeners, and yet there can be no question that our bird is the local representative of the white willow-grouse, which ranges over the whole of Northern Europe. There are absolutely no structural differences between the two. Here is a species, then, which has lost, through disuse, the power of turning white in winter with the absence of the necessity for doing so.

Let us see how the adoption of protective colouring holds as applied to these species—all of which are brown in summer, white in winter. The Iceland falcon and the ptarmigan have pretty much the same habitat, the one preying upon the other. The ptarmigan's plumage during the breeding season is dark brown, even approaching to black; but in autumn, during the transition stage, it is grey, this being the general tint of the mosses and lichens among which it lives. Suppose, however, that the summer bird never changed its plumage, what chance of survival would it stand against its enemies when the ground was covered with snow? Remaining, as it would, a black speck on the otherwise white surface, it would in a few years become extinct. The ptarmigan, then, furnishes an example of the assumption of three different states of plumage, each assimilating to the physical conditions by which it is surrounded. Of course the same rule applies to the falcon, which is also white. Precisely the same set of facts operate in the case of the large snowy owl in the fir countries which it inhabits. Here its food consists of lemmings, Alpine hares, and birds, particularly the willow-grouse and ptarmigan. The balance of nature would be slightly against it, however, in the capture of animals which have assumed protective colouring, and hence we are told that "it has been known to watch the grouse-shooters a whole day for the purpose of sharing the spoil. On such occasions it perches on a high tree, and when a bird is shot skims down and carries it off before the sportsman can get near it." Yet again the same reasoning applies to the beautiful silver fox, which structurally in nowise differs from its red-furred cousin of more southern counties.

Hares, according to the altitude of their range, show almost every degree of variableness betweeen red and white. Our common hare is widely distributed, and to such an extent do varietal forms differ that several distinct species (so called) have been evolved out of one. The extreme forms do seem widely separated, until we connect them with the many intermediate links. It then becomes evident that these differences are, after all, such as may be accounted for by conditions of climate and geographical range. The northern form has thick fur, which inclines to white in winter; the central variety has fur of only moderate thickness, becoming grey in winter; and the southern, thin fur of a deep rufous tinge. The calling of these varieties "species" is simply scientific hair-splitting; though this hardly applies to the true variable or mountain hare. This Alpine form is distributed over the countries within the Arctic Circle, though with us its southern haunt is determined by Scotland and Ireland. Again in this species we have three forms, each mainly characteristic of certain latitudes. The first inhabits warm low-lying countries, and does not change colour in winter; of this the Irish hare is a type. The second, the variety common to Northern Europe, which is grey in summer and purely white in winter; while the third is the Arctic form—white right through the year. The six types are probably all varieties of one species, which, for protection, conform to their own environment; and so successfully do they do this, that the progeny of two pair of mountain hares which in 1854 were turned down in the Faroes might long ago have been counted by thousands. The

Scotch variety of this species, which does not change the colour of its fur in winter, is there called the blue hare.

Another interesting example of creatures which are brown in summer and white in winter is the ermine. This is still a fairly common British fur animal, and the change may therefore be watched without going far afield. In the fur countries of high latitudes the change is universal; while here, except in unusually severe winters, it is only partial. In the Lake District, where we have observed a considerable number of these animals, a purely white one is exceedingly rare, though pied specimens are not at all uncommon. The nearest general approach to whiteness was during the prolonged severity of the winter of 1880-81. The last colour about to vanish is usually a brown stripe, prolonged posteriorly down the back; though when the weather is of extreme severity the whole transition can be brought about within a fortnight. It is not that the summer fur is cast and a new one substituted for it, but that each individual hair changes colour. Cold artificially applied will in time bring about the same results as a naturally severe temperature.

There arrive every year in this country, from the north, flocks of pretty little birds called snow-buntings. They come from within the Arctic Circle, and are so variable in their plumage that naturalists almost despaired of ever getting a characteristic description. Indeed, so much a puzzle did these little strangers offer, that for long they were described by the older naturalists as three different birds. Of course, we now know that the mountain, tawny, and snow bunting are one; and this because they have been obtained in almost every possible stage of transition. They breed upon the summits of the highest hills with the ptarmigan; and like that bird regulate their plumage according to the prevailing aspect of their haunts. In this they succeed admirably, and flourish accordingly.

VI.

ADAPTATION TO HAUNT.

The process of natural selection, tending to the survival of the fittest, would almost invariably seem to use colour as its main working factor. The exemplification of this law is, perhaps, nowhere better seen than in the colouring of animals and birds. In the keen struggle for existence, the creature which conforms most nearly to its environment is the one most likely to survive, and therefore perpetuate its characteristics. For upon the fact that the peculiarities of the parents are reproduced in their offspring depends the whole theory of evolution. This may at first suggest that the generality of animals and birds closely conform to the type of the parent stock, and that therefore there is little chance of variation. But while this is so, it is equally true that when any "sport" occurs this is tenaciously retained providing it possesses any advantages over its neighbours in the struggle for existence. In this way a new type may be set up, differing so far from the original as in time to rank as a species.

The great power of variability in animals and plants is probably not yet fully comprehended. We know, however, from Darwin's experiments how many distinct varieties in the case of pigeons have been produced from the wild blue rock, each showing profound modification, not in colour alone, but also in bone structure. Then there are those which show the development of hoods and frills, and others, again, which have within them the homing instinct to an almost incredible degree. All this, of course, has been brought about by man, mostly by selection, and it serves to show how pliable nature is. What has been done to pigeons applies to domestic animals. Given a few years, any monstrosity can be produced, however extravagant; our shorthorns and blood horses have been produced out of the very sorriest material, and now stand as the idealised types of their kind. And what man does artificially, nature is doing daily, but by slow and sure methods of her own. None but those who have dipped beneath the surface can conceive of the struggle which is going on for existence. Nature's competition is of the keenest kind ; the strongest survive, the weakest go to the wall. Even an object so low in the scale of animal creation as a chrysalis assumes a red coat when it is attached to a bright brick wall, and a grey one when it affixes itself to limestone. This inherent power it has in itself, and those individuals which can most cleverly practise deceit in hiding from birds and other enemies survive and reproduce their kind.

With regard to instances of variability which come under our immediate notice, the red grouse of our moorlands as already mentioned is a striking example. There can now be no doubt that this is the "willow grouse" of the Scandinavian Peninsula. Our indigenous bird found itself in an insular position, and has changed from white to speckled red so as to conform to the colour of the heather; it has also modified the colour of its eggs to suit the changed conditions of its existence. Had it remained white, it would soon have been wiped out of existence by the peregrine and other of the large falcons. There can be no question that bird and animal or insect dons the colour and form best calculated to protect it. Whether this change is conscious to the creature that practises it is beside the main question, and hardly enters into the issue. The process is invariably slow, but if any "accidental sport" occurs which is likely to be of use, it is tenaciously retained, and progress is made at a bound.

Many of our British birds exhibit capital instances of protective colouring, and it is a somewhat striking fact that birds of sombre plumage build open nests, while the brilliantly coloured birds either have covered nests or build in holes in trees.

Returning to sexual colour, the dull summer female plumage which characterises so many ground-feeding birds is all the more remarkable as they are the mates of males for the most part distinguished by unusual brilliancy of plumage. The few exceptions to this rule are of the most interesting nature, and go eminently to prove it. In these exceptions it happens that the female birds are more brightly plumaged than the males. But the remarkable trait comes out that in nearly the whole of these cases the male sits upon the eggs. Now this fact more than any other would seem to indicate that the protection afforded by obscure colouring is directly intended to secure the bird's safety during the long and most critical period of its life. This law of protective colouring, it will be seen, most influences those species which build on the ground, and one or two examples may be adduced from our own avifauna, as in the case of the rare dotterel, which breeds on the fells. In winter the colouring of the sexes in this species is almost identical ; but when the breeding season comes round, the female dons a well-defined and comparatively conspicuous plumage, while it is found that the dull-coloured male alone sits upon the eggs.

Mr. Wallace has pointed that the bee-eaters, mot-mots, and touchans—among the most brilliant of tropical or semi-tropical birds—all build in holes in trees. In each of these cases there is hardly any difference in the plumage of the sexes, and where this is so the above rule is almost invariable. Again, our native kingfisher affords an illustration. Woodpeckers, many of which are brightly coloured above, build in the boles of trees, and our own titmice, with their exquisite tints, construct domed nests. Visitors to the Zoological Gardens in Regent's Park will have noticed that the orange-plumaged orioles have pensile nests, which is a characteristic of the order to which they belong, most of the members of which are conspicuous. Bird enemies come from above rather than below, and it will be noticed that the modifications referred to all have reference to the upper plumage. Protective colouring, having for its object the preservation of the species which adopt it, will be found to enter more or less into the economy of every animal and bird and insect in a state of nature ; and therefore it will be seen that there is a general harmony between the colours of an animal and those of its habitation, of which fact almost every living natural object furnishes evidence.

There comes periodically to this country a bird of the starling kind, known as the rose-coloured pastor. It has the back, breast, and sides of an exquisite pale pink; and it is perhaps this bright plumage which prevents it from establishing a residence here. In its continental haunts the bird is observed to affect trees or shrubs bearing rose-coloured flowers, such as the blossoms of the pink azalea, among which the birds more easily escape notice. This is an instance of what is known as adaptive or protective coloration, which we need not go abroad to observe.

The struggle for existence among plants and animals is a hard one, and every point gained in the direction tends to survival. The modification in the forms and colours of insects, and the successful shifts thereby made to elude their enemies, provide the striking facts of the case. Birds modify and rearrange the colours of their plumage, adapt the coloration of their eggs, and the structure and material of their nests, all to the same end. We know that the more highly organised flowers have changed form and colour to satisfy their insect visitors, while the insects themselves have modified their organs so as to enable them the better to visit certain flowers.

In Sumatra Mr. Wallace found a large butterfly its upper surface of a rich purple and with a broad bar of deep orange crossing each wing. The species is found in dry woods and thickets, and when on the wing is very conspicuous, Among the bush and dry leaves the naturalist was never able to capture a specimen; for, however carefully he crept to the spot where the insect had settled, he could never discover it until it suddenly started out again. But upon one occasion he was fortunate enough to note the exact spot where the butterfly settled, and, although it was lost sight of for some time, he at length discovered it close before his eyes. In its position of repose it exactly resembled a dead leaf attached to a twig.

So in our own country we may observe that the purple emperor butterfly affects certain of the brightly coloured wild geraniums, upon which, in repose it is almost impossible to detect it. The brown-spotted fritillaries of our birch woods also offer examples of this class, it being difficult to detect them against the fungus-pitted leaves of every shade of brown and dun and yellow.

VII.

HOW THE WORLD IS FERTILISED.

In approaching the subject of the geographical distribution of animals and plants, one is struck with the marvellous methods which nature adopts for the dispersal of her types. If the seeds of forest trees were merely shed to the ground immediately beneath, they would be in an environment precisely the least likely to further the reproduction of their kind. Instead of this, many of the seeds of forest trees are furnished with wings, an adaptation which allows them to be easily wafted by the wind, and thus fits them for wide dispersal. It is only by possessing some such advantage as this that certain species could survive at all. It is true that acorns and other kindred fruits do not possess this advantage, but then they are largely fed upon by birds, and birds, as will presently be shown, are an admirable means of dispersal. The crop of a wood-pigeon, which burst when the bird fell to the ground when shot, was found to contain sixty-seven acorns, besides a number of beech mast and leaves of clover. In this connection imagine the possible rate of multiplication which would follow the accidental dissemination of a single head of red poppy. If left undisturbed it would, under ordinarily favourable circumtances, ripen forty thousand seeds, each capable of producing a successor. It has been stated by a competent authority that one red poppy could produce plants enough in less than seven years to occupy every inch of the thirty and odd million acres of the United Kingdom.

Ocean currents have not unfrequently been the means of connecting the floras of different continents, and seeds and fruit are sometimes picked up on the western coasts of Britain which have been wafted across the whole Atlantic Ocean. It is also known that certain birds of long and sustained powers of flight cross the Atlantic unaided, and what this may possibly mean will presently be shown. Even land animals are known to cross straits between island and island upon rafts—drift-wood or bits of floating bark.

A quaint instance of transportation of fish spawn is given by an old writer. Izaak Walton believed that pike were bred from pickerel-weed; though he seems to have had some suspicion of this piece of unnatural history, and qualifies his statement by saying that if it is not so "they are brought into some ponds some such other ways as is past man's finding out." But one of his contemporaries attacks this heterodoxy, and " propounds a rational conjecture of the heron-shaw." He thinks it quite likely that while fishing the heron might "lap some spawn about her legs, in regard to adhering to the segs and bull-rushes near the shallows, as myself and others without curiosity, have observed. And this slimy substance adhering to her legs, and she mounting the air for another station, in all probability mounts with her. When note, the next pond she haply arrives at, possibly she may leave the spawn behind her," an observation now known to be strictly accurate. Herons are not the only birds which are aids to dispersal. Although the feet of birds are generally clean, Darwin in one case removed sixty-one grains, and in another twenty-two grains, of dry argillaceous earth from the foot of a partridge, and in the earth there was a pebble as large as the seed of a vetch. The same naturalist had sent to him by a friend the leg of a woodcock, with a little cake of dry earth attached to the shank, and weighing only nine grains ; this contained seeds of the toad-rush, which not only germinated but flowered. But perhaps the most interesting case of all was that of a red-legged partridge forwarded by Professor Newton. This had been wounded, and was unable to fly ; and a ball of hard earth adhered to it, weighing six and a half ounces. The earth had been kept for three years, but when broken and watered, and placed under a bell-glass, no fewer than eighty-two plants sprang from it.

American passenger pigeons are frequently captured in the State of New York with their crops still filled with the undigested grains of rice that, according to Mr. Howard Saunders, must have been taken in the distant fields of Georgia and South Carolina, apparently proving that the birds had passed over the intervening space within a few hours. It is known that at certain seasons thousands of these beautiful pigeons are killed, not only by man, but by predatory animals and birds; and their long migratory journeys as a possible means of dispersal becomes at once evident. As bearing on this particular subject, Darwin has proved that the hard seeds of fruit pass uninjured through even the digestive organs of a turkey. In the course of two months he picked up in his garden twelve kinds of seeds out of the excrement of small birds which seemed perfect, and some of them germinated. The crops of birds do not secrete gastric juice, and consequently do not in the least injure germination. Darwin forced many kinds of seeds into the stomachs of dead fish, and then gave them to fishing eagles, storks, and pelicans in the Zoological Gardens. The birds, after long intervals, either ejected the seeds in pellets or passed them; after which several kinds still retained the power of germination. In the tropics countless swarms of locusts sometimes suddenly make their appearance, and as suddenly vanish. They cover every leaf-bearing thing, and occasionally denude whole districts of their greenery. So great are their powers of flight that they have been seen at sea nearly four hundred miles from nearest land. In Natal the farmers, rightly or wrongly, believe that the locusts introduce injurious seeds upon their grass lands, and the following would seem to show that their belief is well founded. A Mr. Weale, who was in their way of thinking, collected a packet of dried pellets and sent them to England. When closely examined under the microscope they revealed a number of tiny seeds from which plants of seven kinds of grasses were ultimately raised.

In comparatively few years a small island in mid ocean had quite an important addition to its flora, merely from the fact that the grave of an officer was dug with a spade that had been used in England. The seeds from which these sprang were embedded in the dry earth adhering to the spade. Floating driftwood is quite an important means of dispersal, as can easily be understood; and the natives of some of the coral islands in the Pacific procure stones for their tools solely from the roots of drifted trees, the stones being a valuable royal tax. In this connection Darwin made the following interesting experiments. He found that when irregularly-shaped stones were embedded in the roots of trees, small parcels of earth were frequently enclosed in their interstices or behind them, so perfectly that not a particle could be washed away during the longest transport. Out of one small portion of earth thus completely enclosed by the roots of an oak about fifty years old three dicotyledonous plants germinated. It is well known that in many cases a few days' immersion in sea-water is sufficient to kill seeds, but a number taken out of the crop of a pigeon which had floated on the water for thirty days nearly all germinated. Other aids to dispersal already referred to are wading birds, which frequent the muddy edges of ponds, and, if suddenly flushed, would be the most likely to have muddy feet. "Birds of this order wander more than those of any other, and they are occasionally found on the most remote and barren islands of the open ocean; they would not be likely to alight on the surface of the sea, so that any dirt on their feet would not be washed off; and when gaining the land they would be sure to fly to their natural fresh-water haunts. I do not believe," says Darwin, "that botanists are aware how charged the mud of ponds is with seeds; I have tried several little experiments, but will here only give the most striking case. I took in February three tablespoonfuls of mud from three different points, beneath water, on the edge of a little pond; this mud when dried weighed only six and three-quarter ounces. I kept it covered up in my studio for six months, pulling up and counting each plant as it grew. The plants were of many kinds, and were altogether five hundred and thirty-seven in number; and yet the viscid mud was all contained in a breakfast cup. Considering these facts, I think it would be an inexplicable circumstance if water birds did not transport plants to unstocked ponds and streams, situate at very distant points. The same agency may have come into play with the eggs of some of the smaller fresh-water animals."

The manner in which the ubiquitous brown rat obtrudes itself everywhere is only paralleled by the like qualities in the British sparrow. Our weeds have migrated to the colonies, and certain kinds have almost overrun them. In New Zealand the common dock is now widely disseminated, the original seeds being sold by a lively British tar as those of the tobacco plant.

THE END.

PRINTED BY NICHOLS AND SONS, 25, PARLIAMENT STREET WESTMINSTER.

"A pleasant little book for anglers and lovers of nature."—Saturday Review.

BRITISH SPORTING FISHES.

By JOHN WATSON.   Crown 8vo, 3s. 6d.

From the GLOBE.

"The papers it contains treat of salmon, trout, grayling, pike, perch, and most fresh-water fish. There are pleasant chapters on silvers streams and good practical essays on the depopulation and restocking of trout streams, water and fish poachers, ephemeræ, and above all a useful article on fish stews."

From the SPEAKER.

"Naturalists as well as anglers will find Mr. Watson's remarks about 'British Sporting Fishes' quite worthy of their attention. The book is written by a man who has mastered the wily tactics of salmon, pike, trout, perch, carp, and bream, and knows how to bait a tempting hook for each and all of them. The 'small fry' of lake and river are not forgotten by Mr. Watson, and two of the most interesting chapters in a lively volume are devoted to roach, minnow, stickleback and other little fish."

From the SATURDAY REVIEW.

"A pleasant little book for anglers and lovers of nature is Mr. John Watson's 'British Sporting Fishes.' All fresh-water fish that afford any sort of sport are sporting fish according to the author, who finds room in his delightful sketches of the life-histories and habitats of fish for the smallest of small fry, the roach, the minnow, the stickleback, and so forth. Mr. Watson's sketches follow a downward scale, from salmon and trout to the small fry of the pool and the brook, and all are characterized by remarkable delicacy of observation."

From the MORNING POST.

"'Sketches of British Sporting Fishes,' by John Watson, afford pleasant reading interspersed with information, the result of practical experience and close observation. Nor does the author confine his remarks entirely to fish, but touches on such connected subjects as fish poaching, some of the tricks of which he describes. The chapter on grayling is written in the same easy and unpretentious style as the rest of the book."

Jnited Kingdom
ource UK Ltd.
)1B/257/A